13.99

NVQ/SVQ
Workbook, Level 3

FOOD PREPARATION
and COOKING

To be used in conjunction with *Advanced Practical Cookery*
and also *The Theory of Catering* and *Practical Cookery*

WITHDRAWN

Victor Ceserani, Ronald Kinton
and David Foskett

Hodder & Stoughton

A MEMBER OF THE HODDER HEADLINE GROUP

A catalogue record for this title is available from the British Library.

ISBN 0 340 61857 4

First published 1995
Impression number 10   9   8   7   6   5   4   3   2   1
Year   1999   1998   1997   1996   1995

Typeset by Wearset, Boldon, Tyne and Wear.
Printed in Great Britain for Hodder & Stoughton Educational, a division of Hodder Headline Plc, 338 Euston Road, London NW1 3BH by Bath Press Ltd, Avon.

Contents

Introduction   iv

Managing Resources and the Environment   **1**
Unit 3B2   Control the receipt, storage and issue of resources   3
Unit 3D1   Monitor and maintain the health, safety and security of workers,   16
             customers and other members of the public

Patisserie and Confectionery   **23**
Unit 3F1   Produce hot and cold sweets   25
Unit 3F2   Prepare and produce pastry products   55
Unit 3F3   Prepare and process fermented dough products, sponges and cake   69
             products
Unit 3F4   Produce pastillage, marzipan, chocolate and sugar products   95

Kitchen and Larder Work   **119**
Unit 3F5   Prepare and cook complex fish and shellfish dishes   121
Unit 3F6   Prepare and cook complex meat, offal, game and poultry dishes   157
Unit 3F7   Prepare, cook and finish hot sauces, soups and cold dressings   210
Unit 3F8   Prepare, cook and finish complex vegetable dishes   240
Unit 3F9   Prepare, cook and present cold buffet items   266

Introduction

The aim of this book is to develop the candidate's underpinning knowledge in order to carry out the competence required to achieve NVQ/SVQ level 3 in Catering Hospitality, Food Preparation and Cooking. It is intended solely for the candidate's own use and self-assessment.

In addition to learning the skills of food preparation and cooking, it is necessary to develop an inquiring mind, a knowledge of the commodities used and the reasons why practical work is carried out in certain ways. In other words, the theory of food and cooking.

The purpose of this workbook is to assist students in developing a systematic approach to combining theory with practice, which is essential for a proper understanding of the skills involved.

Candidates are advised to develop an attitude of mind so that, whenever working in practical situations, they are always thinking *why* the various processes are used and *about* the commodities. Similarly, when working through this book, they should be thinking of the practical situation in relation to the theory.

Never separate theory and practice in the mind – the two should at all times complement each other to develop a helpful, deeper understanding.

National and Scottish Vocational Qualifications (NVQ/SVQ)

A National or Scottish Vocational Qualification is awarded following a method of assessment to candidates achieving the required level of ability. These levels are:

- level 1: Operative
- level 2: Craft
- level 3: Supervisory
- level 4: Junior management

Assessment occurs at work, and/or college in a realistic working environment and is available to all irrespective of age and entry qualification requirements. The system enables the participants to progress through the levels in a flexible manner according to individual circumstances and abilities. Previous experience and knowledge are taken into account.

Candidates are fully involved in the assessment procedure by the completion of an evidence diary recording their performance. This provides evidence of activities carried out in a working environment while being assessed.

Understanding, underpinning knowledge or related theory is assessed orally or by the use of visual or other aids and, for levels 3/4, written questions may be used.

Recording assessment details

With all aspects of dealing with training, people's records must always be stored securely and available only to those authorised to have access to them.

- Past records should be valid, accurate relevant and reliable.
- Current information about learners must also be valid, accurate relevant and reliable.
- All interpretation of records must be fair and justified.

The records should be kept together and form the portfolio of evidence and may include audio and video tapes.

It is essential at the outset that all records are retained and may include:

- completed record units;
- assessment plans;
- oral/written questions used during assessment;
- any case studies or role plays used;
- work-based projects;
- accreditation of prior learning assessment plans;
- details of accreditation of prior learning advised or assessed;
- references and letters of validation;
- records of meeting with assessors and verifiers;
- certificates;
- documented feedback given to candidates.

A candidate needs to ensure that the contents of his/her portfolio are relevant to the performance criteria and range of elements being worked towards.

MANAGING RESOURCES AND
THE ENVIRONMENT

Unit 3B2

Control the receipt, storage and issue of resources

3B2.1 *Monitor and control the receipt of goods*

The receiving area is prepared and staff are available to take receipt of deliveries.

1 Who would take receipt of deliveries?

....

2 What preparation is required prior to delivery of goods?

....

Goods received are matched against documented information and discrepancies are identified.

3 What documents are needed on receipt of goods?

....

4 What do you understand by 'discrepancies'?

....

Goods are matched against purchasing specifications and deviations are identified.

5 What is a purchasing specification?

....

6 Give examples of specifications for raspberries and racks of lamb.

....

....

7   What deviations may occur when, for example, raspberries are delivered?

....

Discrepancies and deviations are investigated thoroughly and prompt action is taken to rectify any problems and minimise disruption to operations.

8   What prompt action should be taken?

....

9   Give an example of a typical problem.

....

10   How may disruption be minimised?

....

Goods are transported to the appropriate storage area within the necessary timescale and in accordance with relevant legislation.

11   State why goods on delivery should be quickly taken to the correct storage area.

....

12   What precautions should be taken with:

Frozen foods? ....

Fresh fish? ....

13   What happens to refrigerated storage if the doors are open for a long period of time?

....

Security procedures are fully maintained.

14   Who is responsible for the security of goods?

....

15 What procedures would be taken in an organisation to prevent the stealing of goods?

....

16 Does a system of documentation help to prevent pilfering? If so, explain how.

....

17 What should you do if you become aware that items are disappearing?
    Report it to your immediate superior?
    Call the police?
    Do nothing?
    Check the organisation's policy in such matters?

3B2.2 *Control the storage of stocks/goods*

The storage of perishable items, non-perishable items and hazardous items in any establishment must be thorough. Legal requirements must be complied with regarding safety and hygiene. Goods must be secure to prevent stealing and an effective system of control to prevent wastage, over-ordering and under-ordering should be in force.

Items of a hazardous nature must be kept secure. This applies particularly to certain cleaning items, for example, bleach, ammonia, disinfectants and oven cleaners.

Checks on all items are essential. These may be spot checks taken at random for particular items to see that records are accurate, as well as a full stock audit to check all the goods in store. The information obtained identifies losses and deterioration, as well as inappropriate ordering. Having too much of an item is not practising economy effectively; however, purchasing in bulk may be economical provided storage space is not a problem.

Storage facilities are fully prepared and maintained under the correct conditions.

1 For correct storage conditions other than hygiene, give two examples and explain why you have stated them.

....

....

2 Explain what you understand by storage facilities being properly maintained.

....

....

3 Name four non-food items and state where they should be stored.

....

....

....

....

4 Name two hazardous items and state how they should be stored.

....

....

5 Explain what you understand by stock rotation and state why it is necessary.

....

6 What policy has your organisation implemented regarding stock rotation?

....

Stock is stored and handled in accordance with product instructions, organisational policy and relevant legislation.

7 Name two different products in your establishment and find out what storage instructions the producers give.

....

....

8 What policy has your organisation regarding complying with the legal requirements of the storage of goods?

....

9 At what temperature should the following equipment be maintained?

Refrigerator: 5°C   Meat cabinet: ....

Fish cabinet: ....   Freezer: ....

Stock rotation procedures are fully maintained.

10 Why is this so important with perishable foods?

....

11 Is rotation of tinned stock necessary? If your answer is 'yes', state why.

....

Deterioration and losses of stock in storage are identified and investigated, the appropriate remedial action is taken and/or reported.

12 Name two commodities which deteriorate and explain why deterioration occurs.

....

....

13 Why may stock be 'lost'?

....

14 Explain how deterioration and loss may be prevented.

....

....

15 What action would you take in your establishment to prevent deterioration?

....

....

Security of stock is maintained by appropriate procedures.

16 What procedure is in force to ensure that stock is secure within your organisation?

....

....

17 Name four of the storekeepers roles with regard to security.

a Accurate record keeping

b ....

c ....

d ....

18 What physical conditions are necessary and what procedures must be complied with to make stores safe and secure?

....

....

19 What do you understand by spot check and full check?

....

....

20 Access to stock and the use of space is optimised. Suggest how access to stock is achieved:
    By the design of stores:

....

    By the siting of stores:

....

    By fittings in stores:

....

21 Who is responsible for using storage space advantageously?

....

Opportunities to improve the storage system are identified and recommendations made to the appropriate authority.

22   In what ways can the existing storage system in your establishment be improved?

....

....

23   To whom would you make recommendations and how would you present them?

....

....

24   If you thought 'sack the storekeeper', how would you express such an idea?

....

Relevant information is accurately recorded in the appropriate format and made available to the appropriate people.

25   Name seven items of information regarding stock that need to be recorded.

a Amount received   **e** ....

b Amount issued   **f** ....

c ....   **g** ....

d ....

26   What system of records exists in your organisation?

....

....

27   Who in your establishment needs to know the details of stock used, stock in hand and stock required?

....

....

28   Name two computer software packages that are available as a food and beverage stock control system.

....

....

29 The key objective of storage is to ensure that an adequate supply of all purchased items is maintained for immediate use, with the minimum loss arising from wastage, spoilage or p..............................

30 In order to ensure the correct storage procedures are followed, it is important that:

   a The stores are well designed, to ensure no access to .... personnel.

   b Shelves are of the .... specification.

   c Each storage area is maintained at the .... temperature.

   d Opening times of some storage areas may be r..............................

31 A key point of the storage function is the maintenance of clerical records. These may be in the form of:

   a Stock book

   b B.......... cards

   c Stock cards

The objective is to accurately record all stock movements in and out of the store.

32 A vital part is ensuring the accuracy of the stock records and the physical stock take.

   This must be done when ....

   and must be independently ....

When the stocktaking process is complete and the appropriate stock levels computed, it is vital to know what the level of stock should be.

33 The optimum stock level should relate directly to the known consumption pattern but should take into account:

   a The maximum consumption of a product against the m.......................... re-order time.

   b the usual length of the re.......................... cycle.

   c The economic .... to be ordered.

d Delivery ....

e Storage .... available

f The shelf .... of ....

g Purchase terms available at the time of ordering.

h Cash .... constraints

i Price .... and .... demand.

3B2.3 *Control of the issue of stock/goods*

Stock/goods are issued on receipt of the appropriate authorisation and/or documentation.

1 What documents are required in your establishment before goods are issued from stores?

....

....

2 Who has authority to:
   Issue goods?

....

   Request goods?

....

3 Are there any restrictions on, for example, specific goods or certain amounts, which may be requisitioned in your organisation?

....

....

4 What information is needed on a requisition form?

....

....

5 What do you understand by countersigned?

....

....

Goods issued match specific requirements.

6 Why should goods issued be the same as those requested?

....

....

7 If items cannot be supplied from stores or only partially supplied, what is the procedure in your establishment?

....

....

Goods are issued in accordance with stock rotation procedures and organisational policy.

8 Who issues goods which are requested and in what order are items issued from stock?

....

....

9 What is the organisational procedure with which you or your colleagues comply?

....

....

Records of issues are complete, accurate and made available to the appropriate people.

10 Who may be responsible for keeping records?

....

11 How must records be kept?

....

....

12 Who has access to records?

....

CONTROL OF SUBSTANCES HAZARDOUS TO HEALTH REGULATIONS 1988

The Control of Substances Hazardous to Health Regulations 1988 (COSHH) came into effect on 1 October 1989 and place a duty on all employers to reduce employee exposure to hazardous substances to within, and preferably below, acceptable limits. The emphasis is on personal, as opposed to environmental, exposure and consideration should be given to skin contact, skin absorption, inhalation and ingestion.

All employers have a duty to ensure comprehensive assessments are carried out for every identifiable substance hazardous to health encountered at work.

13 What should the assessment cover?
   a Identification of all substances hazardous to health associated with the work processes.

   b Employees likely to be ....

   c Degree and length of ....

   d Work areas affected.

   e Existing control m.............................. and their efficiency.

   f Existing monitoring ....

   g Existing provision for in.............................. information and training.

   h Recommendations for any inadequacies.

14 Who should carry out the assessment?

....

<u>3B2.4</u> *Implement the physical stock-take within the area of responsibility*

When presenting information, having made a physical stock-take it may be essential to clarify certain factors. Examples of this could be explanations of why items have been damaged or deteriorated. All items of stock have value, but if they have not yet been paid for, this information should be made known as would items for which a credit note has been issued. Materials and goods used for display, exhibitions, competitions, etc., would be noted and accounted for. Information about future issues needs to be included so as to complete the picture, and orders may be in but not yet issued.

Should stock be transferred to other departments, branches or stores, this information needs to be recorded and passed to those in the establishment who need to be informed. It is essential that the physical stock-take and the records agree. Any reconciliation should be stated so as to explain the discrepancy between actual goods and the stock-take records.

Stock-taking procedures are effectively communicated to the appropriate staff.

1   Why should those persons responsible for stock know what procedures are required of them for stock-taking?

....

....

2   In what form can communication be most effective?

....

Required documentation is made available to the appropriate staff.

3   State three documents which would be required.

....

4   Explain the purpose of these documents.

....

....

....

5 Who may be the appropriate staff requiring the documents?

....

Records of physical stock-take are complete, accurate and up to date.

6 Why should records be accurate, complete and up to date?

....

....

Additional information which will affect stock reconciliation is made available to the appropriate people.

7 Give four examples which may affect stock reconciliation.

....

....

....

....

8 Who may require this information?

....

All relevant information is accurately recorded in a suitable format and made available to the appropriate people.

9 What information is required when stock-taking?

....

Record of Achievement – Completion of Unit 3B2

Candidate's signature   ....

Assessor's signature   ....

Date   ....

Unit 3D1

Monitor and maintain the health, safety and security of workers, customers and other members of the public

3D1.1 *Maintain security/safety procedures in own area of responsibility*

1 How would you identify potential security risks in areas for which you are responsible?

....

....

2 What procedure would you follow, having discovered faults in the security system?

....

....

3 Why is it necessary for employees to be security conscious?

....

....

4 In your establishment, how frequently are inspections carried out regarding security of premises?

....

5 List the potential lapses of security which may occur.

....

....

6   Hazard spotting is necessary to prevent accidents. What hazards can you spot in your working environment?

....

....

7   What procedures do you take to prevent there being hazardous situations?

....

....

8   In the event of an accident occurring, to whom should it be reported and where recorded?

....

....

9   What is the policy in your establishment for ensuring accidents and lapses in security are reported and appropriate action taken?

....

....

10   What details are to be recorded following an accident?

....

....

11   Equipment manufacturers produce instructions for use. What other information may they provide?

....

....

12   Why should manufacturers' guidelines be followed?

....

13 What information should be sited by electrical cutting and slicing equipment?

....

....

14 Who should be informed when there is a serious accident?

....

15 Who is responsible for first aid in your workplace?

....

16 Where is your nearest accident and emergency hospital department?

....

3D1.2 *Monitor and maintain the health and safety of workers, customers and other members of the public*

1 List the categories of people entering the premises who could be at risk where you work.

....

....

2 What potential risks could endanger these people?

....

....

3 What routines occur to ensure that premises are free from hazards and have high standards of hygiene?

....

....

4   How frequently should safety and maintenance checks take place?

....

5   Why should details of an accident be recorded and why should it be legible?

....

....

6   Why should equipment instructions be fully complied with?

....

....

7   What health and safety signs may be required and how should they be displayed?

....

....

8   Explain why maintenance checks are necessary. How are faults rectified and by whom?

....

....

....

....

9   Where in your establishment is the first aid box and what are its contents?

....

....

10   Name two organisations who run first aid courses.

....

....

11 Explain the procedure for treating cuts and burns.

....

....

....

12 State the major causes of accidents in kitchens.

....

....

<u>3D1.3</u> *Maintain a healthy and safe working environment*

1 How do staff in your establishment know the legislation regarding health and safety?

....

2 What methods are employed to ensure compliance with the health and safety legislation?

....

....

3 Explain how hazards can be avoided.

....

....

4 Having obtained a safe and healthy working environment, how can this situation be continued?

....

....

5 Why is training in health and safety essential and what should it include?

....

....

6 Where would you obtain information regarding fire prevention and procedures in the event of a fire?

....

....

7 In the event of a bomb alert, what is your organisation's policy and procedure?

....

....

8 What records regarding health and safety must be kept and what details should they contain?

....

....

....

9 What procedures should occur in the event of:
 a Infestation

....

....

 b Contamination

....

....

10 What happens in your establishment when staff fail to comply with the organisation's standards?

....

....

11 Why is ongoing training regarding health and safety essential?

....

....

12 Explain why all areas accessible to staff and other persons must be safe.

....

....

Record of Achievement – Completion of Unit 3D1

Candidate's signature   ....

Assessor's signature   ....

Date   ....

PATISSERIE AND
CONFECTIONERY

Unit 3F1

Produce hot and cold sweets

3F1.1 *Prepare hot sweets*
3F1.2 *Cook and finish hot sweets*

Food hygiene is essential when working in the pastry and bakery environment.

1 State six basic principles of food hygiene that you observe when working in this
   department.
   Example All items are stored correctly in accordance with the required legislation.

   ....

   ....

   ....

   ....

   ....

   ....

2 Employees are also responsible for safety under the Health and Safety Act. Outline
   how you implement the safety policy within the department.

   ....

   ....

3 Name three processes in the pastry kitchen which are most likely to kill food
   poisoning bacteria.

   ....

   ....

   ....

4 A classical apple charlotte is unmoulded and served hot. What precautions have to be taken in order that the product does not collapse on unmoulding?

....

....

5 Name six hot sweets with which you are familiar.

....

....

....

6 Describe the preparation, cooking and service of two of the above sweets. Sketch the suitable plate service of one of the described sweets.

7 Soufflés, pudding soufflé, soufflé pancakes are all aerated hot sweets. What is meant by aerated?

....

8 What is a panada?

....

9 How are the following flavours added to a panada for soufflé?
Chocolate:

....

Grand Marnier:

....

Coffee:

....

10 What is added to egg white in order to strengthen it, e.g. for beating?

....

11 How does a pancake differ from a waffle?

....

12 List six pancake fillings and three waffle fillings.

....

....

....

....

....

13 Maple syrup is often served with waffles, but what is maple syrup?

....

14 At what temperature should a four-portion soufflé be cooked?

....

15 Describe a soufflé of your own choice, one which you have prepared or have seen prepared in your establishment, which is not a classical recipe.

....

....

16 Why is strong flour used in the production of apple strudel?

....

17 Name three variations to apple strudel.

....

....

18 Give the recipe based on four to six portions for a classical steamed sponge pudding.

....

....

....

19 Describe four hot sweets using steamed sponge pudding mix for plated service which do not follow classical lines. Illustrate your answer with sketches.

20 Name the various types of rice used for hot sweets.

....

21 How does a French rice pudding differ from a traditional English rice pudding?

....

22 Describe four hot sweets with which you are familiar where the main ingredient is cereal based.

....

....

....

....

23 Suggest a suitable rice-, semolina- or tapioca-based hot sweet which could be suitable for banquet service. How would you serve it for 250 people?

....

....

24 Describe how hot sweets may be modified to take account of healthy eating.

....

....

25 Outline the quality control points essential when writing standardised recipes for hot sweets.

  a Purchasing; specification of ingredients correct.

  b Preparation procedures; correct storage temperature; handling.

  c ....

  d ....

  e ....

  f ....

26 Give examples of hot sweet dishes which use the following preparations.

Preparation	Hot sweet
Creaming	Steamed sponge pudding ....
Use of moulds	Pudding soufflé ....
Folding	Omelette soufflé Jalousie ....
Incorporating fat	Apple turnover ....
Aeration	French rice pudding ....

27 Outline the main contamination threats that are likely when preparing hot sweets.

....

....

....

28 What storage precautions should be taken when preparing uncooked hot sweets?
   a That they are stored at the correct temperature.

   b ....

   c ....

   d ....

29 Name a hot sweet which may be finished by one of the following methods:

Finish	Hot sweet
Grilling	Flan viennoise
Turning out, de-moulding	
Cooling	
Glazing	
Coating	
Filling	Pancakes
Piping	
Dipping	
Sprinkling	
Portioning	Apple strudel

30 State the common faults often to be found in the following sweets:

Hot sweet	Common faults
Soufflé	Oven too cool Insufficient beating of egg whites Overbeating of egg whites ....

Hot sweet	Common faults
Rice pudding	Ingredients weighed incorrectly; too much rice giving a heavy, stodgy texture ....
Sponge puddings	Mixture too wet ....
Choux paste fritters	Deep-frying oil not at correct temperature ....
Apple fritters	Batter runs off; apple ring should have been passed through flour then batter ....

31   Suggest a different hot sweet which may be produced from the following fruits:

Fruit	Hot sweet
Fresh strawberries	
Fresh rhubarb	
Fresh blackcurrants	
Fresh gooseberries	
Fresh peaches	
Dried apricots	
Fresh mangoes	

32 With two of the fresh fruits and the hot sweets you have listed in question 31, describe their preparation, cooking, finish and service.

....

....

....

....

3F1.3 *Prepare cold sweets*

3F1.4 *Process and finish cold sweets*

1 Outline four main hygiene procedures which have to be followed when preparing cold sweets relevant to current legislation.
Example Due care is taken to make sure that all risk of contamination is minimised through careful handling, preparation and storage of raw materials.

....

....

....

....

....

2 How should cold sweets which contain large amounts of fresh cream be stored?

....

....

....

3 Name a cold sweet using each of the following preparation methods.

Preparation method	Cold sweet
Creaming	
Folding	
Aeration	Cold lemon soufflé
Using the addition of flavours and colours	
Combining	

4 Describe the method of preparation and service of two of the sweets and give the amounts for 20 covers.

....

....

....

....

....

....

....

5 Gelatine is a natural setting agent produced from collagen. Give a vegetarian alternative.

....

6 Fonds are commercial mousse preparations which are ideally suited to bulk production. These fonds often use a mixture of setting agents to give a smooth high-quality mouth feel gel. Name four different setting agents used in fonds.

....

....

7   Describe the use of jaconde mixture in the production of cold sweets.

....

....

8   Either draw the presentation of one sweet you have produced recently from a jaconde mixture, or using your creativity and imagination create a sweet using the mixture.

9   State the reasons for using silpat mats in preference to silicone paper when making two-coloured jaconde biscuits.

....

....

10   Why is it necessary to adjust the recipe for a chocolate bavarois if using a 70–72 per cent cocoa solids couverture in place of cooking chocolate?

....

....

11 When making a classic chocolate mousse with a pastry cream base and high in chocolate content, what adjustments would you make to ensure a soft and light texture?

....

....

12 Create two cold sweets suitable for banquet service from the following list only: flour, butter, eggs, sugar, milk, honey, yoghurt, cream cheese, gelatine, flaked almonds, liqueur, fresh pears, apples, mangoes, fresh coconut. Draw the presentation and list the ingredients and method for four portions.

13 Give a costing for one of the sweets.

Name of dish:			Four portions	
Ingredients	Amount	Cost per unit	Cost	
			£	p
		Total cost		
		Cost of one portion		

14 Name six items made in the pastry kitchen using rice grains.
Example Imperial rice (*Riz à l'impératrice*)

a .... d ....

b .... e ....

c .... f ....

15 List the ingredients of two of the dishes you have mentioned in question 14 and describe the method of production.

....

....

....

....

....

....

....

....

16 State the name of the enzyme in pineapple which reacts with gelatine, making the production of mousse using fresh pineapple and gelatine impossible.

....

17 Describe the action of this protolytic enzyme and gelatine.

....

....

18 Name four cold sweets using meringue.
Example   Vacherin aux fruits

a ....   **c** ....

b ....   **d** ....

19 State the hygiene principles which must be observed when producing meringue.

....

....

20 Why is lemon juice, tartaric acid or acetic acid sometimes added to egg white for the production of meringues?

....

21 How are meringue nests prepared and cooked?

....

....

22 Why may egg white powder be added to egg white for the production of meringue?

....

23 State the hygiene and safety principles that must be observed when using eggs for cold sweets.

....

....

24 If you were inducting an apprentice in the pastry department, outline the safety procedures you would expect him/her to observe; in particular, explain the food safety procedures relating to fresh cream and the finishing of cold sweets.

....

....

....

....

....

....

....

....

....

....

....

....

....

....

25 Describe the process required in the production of:
Cream-based ice-cream:

....

....

A fruit-based water ice:

....

....

26 List all the ingredients required and describe the making and serving of a red wine sorbet and a red wine granité. Describe the difference between a sorbet and a granité.

....

....

....

....

....

....

27 Draw and label a two-flavoured ice-cream bombe.

28   List the ingredients for a pâte à bombe.

....

....

....

....

29   Show how a pâte à bombe can be used in the making of either a biscuit glacé or soufflé glacé.

....

....

30   Using your creativity, describe by use of a diagram how you would present a biscuit glacé or a soufflé glacé to ensure ease of service and efficient cost/portion control.

31   Ice-cream is a complex emulsion. What is meant by the term emulsion?

....

32   Why is glycerol monostearate added to commercial ice-cream and which substance is used for the same purpose if ice-cream is produced in the pastry department.

....

....

33 Outline the food safety requirements which must be applied to the preparation, production and service of ice-cream goods.

....

....

34 State why fruit/water ice does not freeze to a firm state.

....

35 Explain what causes the granular texture of ice-cream.

....

36 Give a recipe for a cold cheesecake and list six different types of toppings which you are familiar with.

....

....

....

....

....

....

....

37 State the difference between a Chartreuse and a Charlotte.

....

....

38 Name three Chartreuses and three Charlottes with which you are familiar; briefly describe each.

Chartreuse	Description	Charlotte	Description
Banana	Mould lined with lemon jelly, topped with sliced banana, filled with vanilla bavarois	Russe	Mould lined with biscuit à la cuillère, filled with vanilla bavarois

39 Name two cold sweets that use the following basic pastes, giving a brief description. One example for each is given.

Paste	Sweet	Description
Choux paste	Salambos	Large bun filled with rum pastry cream topped with caramel
Puff pastry	Millefeuille	Layers of puff paste filled with cream and fruit
Sweet paste	Pear flan	Sweet paste flan cooked blind, filled with pastry cream and pears glazed with suitable flan jelly

Paste	Sweet	Description
Sablé paste	Raspberry sablé	Rounds of sablé paste filled with raspberries and cream

40 From the following lists, either name or create cold sweets using fresh fruit and pastry.

Fruit

Apples

Blackcurrants

Kiwi

Pineapple

Raspberries

Pastes

Short

Sweet

Choux

Puff

Sablé

41 Describe two sweets from your answer in question 40, the method of preparation, cooking and serving. Suggest if the sweets mentioned are suitable for banquet service.

....

....

....

....

....

....

....

....

42   Name a cold sweet which may be produced from the following process methods.

Process method	Sweet
Freezing	Biscuit glacé
Boiling	
Baking	
De-moulding	
Refrigeration	

43   Name a cold sweet that may be finished by the following methods:

Finishing method	Cold sweet
Cooling	
Stacking	
Glazing	Crème brulée
Cutting	
Filling	Profiteroles
Piping	Bavarois
Portioning	

44   Name four sweets which can be produced from eggs, milk, cream and sugar using the process poaching *au bain marie.*

....

....

45   Poaching *au bain marie* using the ingredients in question 44 requires special attention during the cooking process. Why?

....

....

46   What is meant by syneresis?

....

47 State how the ingredients for cold sweets can be adjusted to comply with healthy eating guidelines.

....

....

48 Create or modify two existing cold sweet dishes to make them more attractive to the health conscious customer.

....

....

....

....

3F1.5 *Produce sauces, fillings and coatings*

1 Describe the method of making sauce anglaise and state to what degree it must be heated to conform to the current legislation.

....

....

....

....

2 Pastry cream is also sometimes known as confectioners custard. This filling is used for several sweets, it is often flavoured with liqueurs. Name four cold sweets which use pastry cream as a filling, stating if any additional flavours or liqueurs are added to the cream.

Sweet	Pastry cream flavour
Banana flan	Rum pastry cream

3 The filling for a classical gâteau St Honoré is known as a crème chibouste. Describe a crème chibouste and state the required process for the inclusion of egg white.

....

....

....

....

4 Name four items which can be added to fresh cream before sale to the public in accordance with the Cream Regulations 1970.

....

....

5 Describe how starch forms a gel. Name the best starch for use in a jam sauce and give reasons for this.

....

....

6 What are pectins?

....

....

7 What are alginates?

....

....

8 Give an example of the use of alginates in pastry. Relate your answer to a filling, sauce or coating.

....

....

9   Give an example of using a sabayon in hot or cold sweets.

   ....

10   State the hygiene precautions and procedures which have to be considered when preparing a sabayon. Mention in your answer temperature control and storage.

   ....

   ....

   ....

11   Describe the production of fruit coulis, and outline the different preparation from producing a coulis from hard and soft fruit.

   ....

   ....

   ....

   ....

12   Suggest a suitable fruit coulis to serve with the following sweets.

Sweet	Coulis
Millefeuille filled with fresh raspberries	
Mango and coconut mousse	
Vacherin filled with marron glacé	
Sablé biscuit filled with kiwi and orange segments, topped with crisp caramel	
Hot vanilla and almond soufflé	
Steamed orange sponge pudding	
Hot glazed peaches wrapped in filo pastry	
Apple and cherry strudel	

13   Complete the recipe for boiled butter cream.

   2 eggs
   50 g (2 oz) icing sugar
   300 g (12 oz) granulated sugar
   100 g (4 oz)
   50 g (2 oz)
   400 g (1 lb)

14   To what temperature should the sugar be boiled for boiled butter cream?

....

15   Give three uses of boiled butter cream.

....

....

16   Describe the use of ganache as a filling and as a coating.

....

....

17   By the use of a sketch, suggest a combination of fillings in a sweet/dessert that you are familiar with.

18 Describe how to stabilise and store crème chantilly.

....

....

....

19 Outline the basic principle of jam as a preserve.

....

....

....

20 Give four uses of jam as a filling or topping to hot or cold sweets of your choice.

....

....

....

....

21 What chemical preservative is added to commercial jams.

....

22 List any commercially manufactured fillings that you are aware of.

....

....

....

23 What are the advantages of using a high methoxyl pectin glaze?

....

....

24 Compare a fresh-fruit glaze and a pectin glaze.

....

....

25 Identify the glazes or finishes to the following sweets.

Sweet	Finish
Flan Viennoise	
Apple flan	
Strawberry torte	
Tranche Parisienne	
Dartois aux amandes	
Gâteau Japonaise	

26 Now list six sweets of your own choice. Describe the presentation, filling and finish of each.

Sweet	Presentation	Filling	Finish

27 Coulis are often produced from a process of liquidising and blending. Name a sauce, a filling or coating produced from the following processes.

Reducing: ....

Emulsifying: ....

28 Consider how alternative ingredients may be used to introduce a more healthy eating diet for those who require it. How can the fat content of a filling be reduced?

....

....

....

....

29 Using your creativity and imagination, suggest some suitable sauces from the following ingredients suitable to serve with a range of hot or cold sweets.

Orange juice   Coconut
Earl Grey Tea   Sugar
Whisky   Milk
Eggs   Cream
Honey   Fresh limes
Golden syrup   Passion fruit
Cinnamon   Lychees

....

....

....

....

30 Describe the coating consistency of:
    Ganache:

....

    Butter cream:

....

    Royal icing:

....

31   Why is consistency an important factor in sauce production?

....

....

32   How can each of these be rectified if their consistency is too thin or too thick?

....

....

....

33   When producing coating and fillings, why should the pastry cook be concerned about humidity and temperature?

....

....

34   What are the contamination threats in relation to the making of sauces, filling and coating?

   a Insufficient temperatures reached to destroy bacteria.

   b Pastry cooks contaminating products by poor hygiene techniques.

   c ....

   d ....

   e ....

   f ....

Record of Achievement – Completion of Unit 3F1

Candidate's signature ....

Assessor's signature ....

Date ....

Prepare and produce pastry products

3F2.1 *Prepare and process fresh pastry*
3F2.2 *Cook and finish pastry products*

The method in which fat is added to flour in the production of fresh paste affects the overall finished product.

1   Give an example of a paste which may be produced from each of the following:

Boiling: ....

Rubbing in: ....

Creaming: ....

Lamination: ....

2   Acid is added in the production of puff pastry. The acid acts, upon the gluten, making it more pliable, more extensive, and improving its ability to retain s............................. generated in the baking process; hence pastry is lighter and greater in ....

3   Name the acids which may be added to puff pastry.

....

....

4   In commercial puff pastry, an enzyme is often added in place of an acid to ensure maximum extensibility of the gluten. Name this enzyme.

....

5   Briefly describe how puff pastry rises in the oven.

....

....

6 What is the relationship between the elasticity of the gluten and the resting time?

....

....

7 What do you understand by the term 'hydrogenated fat'?

....

8 Why does puff pastry made with all pastry margarine look white and stale in a much shorter time than paste containing a good percentage of butter?

....

....

9 Describe the different ways of incorporating fat for the production of puff pastry. It is advisable to show this in diagrammatic form.

10 List two effects on the finished product if:
   Puff paste is rolled out in too much flour:

   ....

   Finished puff paste is stored in a warm kitchen:

   ....

   ....

   Dough is firmer than the butter when folding in the butter.

   ....

   ....

11 Name six products which may be produced from short pastry.

   ....

   ....

   ....

12 When making hot water paste, how is the fat incorporated into the flour?

   ....

   ....

13 How does hot water paste differ from raised pie paste in its method of production?

   ....

   ....

14 Why is hot water paste or raised pie paste best for pork and veal fillings?

   ....

   ....

15 Why do pork pies, jellied with agar agar, go off less quickly than those jellied with gelatine or with meat stock?

....

....

16 Give a recipe for a wholemeal short pastry.

....

....

....

....

....

....

....

....

17 List four products where shortening can replace other fats or oils.

....

....

18 Give the factors which control the volume of choux pastry.
   a When choux paste is being baked, any air that has been beaten into it will expand and the water in the paste will be converted into steam.
   b The expanded air as well as the steam tries to escape from the paste but is mostly prevented from doing so because both are trapped and retained within the paste by films of c............................ gluten and unc.............................. films of egg
   ....
   c Egg albumen is extensible and will be in.............................. and distended by the internal .... of the gases .... and ....
   thus the pastries increase a v.............................. and expansion only ceases when the egg albumen films use their extensibility and .... powers.
   However, the moisture which is near to the surface of the paste is driven off fairly quickly, after which the temperature of this water layer of paste, can rise well above the temperature of boiling water.

d During the latter part of this period, and as the paste has already reached very considerable volume, the egg proteins are c............................. and set.

e The volume of the choux pastry goods will depend only slightly upon the strength and extensibility of the gluten of the flour, but very largely upon the gas-holding power of the egg proteins.

19 It is essential to create steam within the paste, under sufficient pressure to aerate as much as possible before coagulation of proteins and surface drying or crust-formation occur. This, however, can only be achieved in what temperature oven?

....

20 Egg albumen is mainly responsible for the ultimate volume of choux paste. Is the strength of the flour of equal importance?

....

21 When making choux paste, why should the eggs never be beaten into the panada until it has been partially or completely cooled?

....

....

22 Why is vol (ammonium carbonate) sometimes added to commercially produced choux paste?

....

....

23 Name four afternoon tea pastries produced from choux pastry.

....

....

24 What is meant by 'fraiser' the paste? What is its purpose?

....

....

25 Give a recipe for sweet pastry using the four ratio numbers which correspond to quantities of ingredients – 8:4:2:1.

....

....

....

....

26 Create a product of your own choice suitable as an afternoon pastry or as a sweet using either puff paste, short paste or sweet paste or a combination of these. Illustrate your answer by use of diagrams.

27 Give the possible reasons for faults which may occur to short pastry.
Hard:

....

....

Soft-crumbly:

....

....

Blistered:

....

....

Soggy:

....

....

Shrunken:

....

....

28 Give the possible reason for faults in puff pastry.
Not flaky:

....

....

Fat oozes out:

....

....

Hard:

....

....

Shrunken:

....

....

Soggy:

....

....

Uneven rise:

....

....

29 Name three uses of sweet paste.

....

....

30 Give the possible reasons for faults in sweet paste.
Heavy and soggy:

....

Tough:

....

31 How should strudel paste be stretched?

....

....

32 Give four uses for sablé paste.

....

....

33 How does noodle paste differ from ravioli paste?

....

....

34 What relationship does strudel paste have with filo paste?

....

....

35 Give four uses for filo paste.

....

....

36 Create a recipe of your own choice using filo paste. The recipe should be suitable for banquet service. Give an outline costing for 10 covers.

....

....

....

....

....

....

....

....

37 Name two types of oven suitable for efficient baking of all pastry and most basic baking products.

....

38 Outline the basic hygiene principles that have to be observed when making fresh pastes.

....

....

....

....

39 Name a paste or product which may be produced using the following preparation methods.

Preparation method	Paste
Mixing	
Folding	Puff pastry Rough puff pastry
Cutting	
Relaxing	All basic pastes
Kneading	
Incorporating fat	All basic pastes
Conducting/chilling	
Scraping down	Sablé paste

40   Using a diagram, show the difference between notching and crimping.

41   From the diagram below, explain what has happened during the baking of the flan case.

....

....

....

....

42 From the following cooking methods, suggest a product that may be produced using fresh paste.

Cooking methods	Product
Baking with filling	Dartois from puff pastry
Steaming	
Boiling/poaching	Gnocchi from choux pastry
Baking blind	
Deep frying	

43 There are many different ways of finishing goods produced from fresh pastry. Name two products which use the following techniques.

Finish	Product
Glazing	
Piping	
Dusting	Apple strudel
Filling	Profiteroles (choux pastry)
Dripping	
Enrobing	
Portioning	Millefeuille (puff pastry)
Use of heat gun	Caramelising Flan viennoise – short pastry

44 Name any other finishing method which you have used which is not listed in question 43.

....

45 What is high ratio fat?

....

46 How does hydrogenated fat differ from high ratio fat?

....

....

47 List the advantages and disadvantages which have to be considered when you purchase commercial paste, such as frozen puff paste.

....

....

....

....

....

....

48 List any commercial paste/products used by your establishment and assess their quality and performance.

....

....

....

....

....

....

49 Explain how recipes for fresh paste may be adapted to make them more 'healthy'.

....

....

50 Suggest ways in which trimmings can be minimised when preparing and using fresh paste.

....

....

51 List any bad practices you have observed in the storage of paste and also in dealing with trimmings.

....

....

....

....

52 Outline the relevant health and safety and food hygiene legislation relating to the production of fresh paste.

....

....

....

....

Record of Achievement – Completion of Unit 3F2

Candidate's signature ....

Assessor's signature ....

Date ....

Prepare and process fermented dough products, sponges and cake products

3F3.1 *Prepare fermented dough products*
3F3.2 *Process and finish fermented dough products*

Yeast goods make use of baker's yeast. Fermentation will only take place with sugar. The flour starch is converted to maltose by flour enzymes which are activated in the presence of water. The maltose is then converted to glucose by maltase which is secreted by the yeast cells. Then other yeast cells convert glucose to carbon dioxide and alcohol. The flour protein undergoes alteration so that the flour will retain the carbon dioxide.

1   Does the size of the starch cells present in flour make any difference to the working of such flour in a dough? Explain fully.

   ....

   ....

   ....

   ....

Viewed through a microscope, a grain of starch will be found to have a very definite shape, but grains from the same source do look similar. For example, a starch cell of wheat is round or slightly oval in shape, and is larger than some of the other kinds of starch, such as rice.

2   What happens to these starch cells when they become moistened and heated?

   ....

   ....

Starches and sugars are carbohydrates which means that they are comprised of three elements, carbon, hydrogen and oxygen, with the latter two elements in proportions necessary to form water. This means that for every atom of oxygen present there will be two atoms of hydrogen. The only difference in the formula for starch and sugar is that the starch contains less water than the sugar, but it is possible to change the former into the latter if it can be induced to take up the extra portion of water.

3   This action is called the hy............................. or sacc............................. of starch.

Dilute acids and some enzymes have the ability to change starch to sugar, and will cause gelatinised starch to combine chemically with extra water so that the starch becomes hydrolysed to sugar.

4   Syneresis is the name given to a particular physical or colloidal change that takes place in starch gels as they age. Give an example of syneresis in relation to flour, yeast and fermentation.

   ....

   ....

5   Both yeast and baking powder produce carbon dioxide gas to aerate the materials with which they are mixed, but why is yeast often used in preference to baking powder?

   ....

   ....

6   Why is salt used in breadmaking?

   ....

7   Yeast is a living organism. By what other name is baker's yeast also known?

   ....

8   Yeast like all other living things must receive sufficient food to enable healthy growth and reproduction to continue. Flour itself normally contains all the foods that are required by yeast for its life and growth. List the conditions required for the yeast to grow and reproduce.

   ....

   ....

In a ferment, the yeast acting upon the sugars produces carbon dioxide which first dissolves in the water to produce carbonic acid. When the water is saturated with the gas, further supplies of the gas become enmeshed by the strands of gluten contained in the ferment, blowing them up into tiny balloons. The continued increase in the quantity of gas aerates the whole of the ferment and slowly inflates it. The increasing of the bulk will continue until, in the case of the ferment, the expansion of the gluten becomes so great that it cannot stretch any further. As the supply of gas is still continuing, the tiny balloons burst.

9 What happens to the ferment?

....

....

10 Why is dough kept covered with a cloth or, preferably, polythene?

....

....

11 Why should you use rice dust instead of flour when moulding dough?

....

....

12 Why is it that bun doughs which contain excessive fat and sugar do not produce satisfactory results?

....

....

13 Why do bun products sometimes acquire a wrinkled surface skin after baking?

....

....

14 Explain why bun goods masked with sugar syrup direct from the oven do not become soaked but acquire a shiny, slightly sticky surface.

....

....

15 Why are fat, sugar and fruit not worked into the dough which is required for dough products until the dough has reached its full state of ripeness?

....

....

16 List the main stages of manufacture for the following doughs:
   Bun dough by direct method:

....

....

....

   Bread roll dough by ferment and dough:

....

....

....

17 Describe the texture and general appearance of bread rolls if:
   Made with soft cake flour:

....

....

   The dough is processed green:

....

....

18 With regard to yeast doughs, briefly describe the following terms:
   BFT and ADD:

....

....

   Ripeness:

....

....

Optimum dough temperature:

....

....

19 Give two examples of laminated yeast doughs.

....

20 Describe the difference in strong flour, wholemeal and soft flour.

....

....

21 Describe the following processing techniques:
Developing the dough:

....

....

Proving the dough:

....

....

Knocking back the dough:

....

....

Dividing the dough:

....

....

Extracting the dough:

....

....

Sheeting and cutting the dough:

....

....

Retarding the dough:

....

....

22 Draw the piece of equipment known as a 'retarder'.

23 Give the method for brioche.

125 ml (¼ pt) milk
25 g (1 oz) yeast
450 g (1 lb 2 oz) strong flour
25 g (1 oz) castor sugar
pinch of salt
50 g (2 oz) butter or margarine
4 eggs
2 g malt extract
zest of 1 lemon
150 g (6 oz) butter or margarine

....

....

....

....

....

....

24 Give three uses of brioche paste.

....

....

25 Using 600 g (1 lb 8 oz) bread flour, give the remainder of the ingredients for croissant.

....

....

....

....

....

....

26 With the use of diagrams, describe the technique of producing the croissant shape.

27 Give a basic recipe for Danish pastry dough.

....

....

....

28 List six types of Danish pastries.

....

....

29 Describe the production of three of the Danish pastries you have named.

....

....

....

....

....

....

30 List the major common faults associated with the production of yeast doughs.
  a Insufficient yeast development.

  b Under proving.

  c ....

  d ....

  e ....

  f ....

  g ....

  h ....

31 Chollo bread is a traditional Jewish bread. It takes the form of a plait. Listed below is the technique for a four-strand plait. Give the order of sequence for a five-strand plait.

4 strand plait	**5 strand plait**
2 over 3	....
4 over 2	....
1 over 3	....

32 Give a recipe for a fermented batter.

....

....

....

33 Suggest four uses of a yeast batter.

....

....

34 List the main contamination threats likely to occur when preparing and storing fermented dough products. Suggest how to minimise these risks.

Main Contamination Threats	How to Minimise Risks
Stored in the wrong refrigerator with high odour products that are likely to taint dough.	Store in correct refrigerator away from foods which are likely to taint.

35 Name a yeast product which uses the following finishing methods.

Finishing method	Fermented product
Moulding	
Cutting	
Dusting	Cream buns
Addition of seeds	Bread rolls
Shaping	
Plaiting	Chollo bread
Piping	
Glazing	

36 Discuss ways in which wastage can be minimised during the production of fermented products.

....

....

....

37 State how equipment, small equipment and preparation surfaces should be dealt with when handling fermented goods in line with current legislation.

....

....

....

....

....

....

3F3.3 *Prepare sponge and cake products*
3F3.4 *Process and finish sponge and cake products*

1 Why is it essential to use good-quality, medium soft flour in the making of slab cakes by the flour or sugar batter methods?
 a This type of flour has the requisite quality and quantity of gluten.

 b ....

2 A flour having too high a percentage of gluten in its composition will cause unsightly cracks to appear across the tops of baked slab cakes and will make them tough. What type of texture will they have?

....

3 What effect would too low a percentage of gluten have on the slab cakes?

....

4 Why is a cake made with all butter not as good as a cake made with part butter and part 100 per cent fat?

....

....

5 Cake batters sometimes curdle. Why is this?

....

....

6 Why is greaseproof paper treated with a solution of silicone resins now used extensively in baking?

....

....

7 Why must the ingredients contained in a cake mixing be balanced?

....

....

8 What are the effects of the following on a cake mixing?
   Too much baking powder:

....

....

   Too much sugar:

....

....

   Too much liquid:

....

....

9 What three effects does sugar have on a cake apart from as a sweetener?
   a Moistening agent.

   b ....

   c ....

10 When baking cakes, what happens if they are moved or knocked while in the oven?

....

....

11 Give three reasons why cakes sometimes sink in the middle.
Example Cake removed from oven before thoroughly cooked.

....

....

....

12 What makes high ratio cake flour different from ordinary flour?

....

....

13 One of the commonest faults with cherry and fruit cakes is that the fruit sinks to the bottom. Give reasons for this.

....

....

....

....

14 What effect do ground almonds have on the prevention of fruit sinking when cake mixing?

....

....

15 What else can be added to the cake mixing to prevent fruit from sinking?

....

16 As soon as cakes are placed in a hot oven, the heat melts the fats – first on the outside, then in the middle. At the same time the air cells begin to expand and if baking powders are present carbon dioxide is released, slowly at first, from the outside to the inside. What happens to the starch cells as the temperature rises?

....

17 List advantages of having the oven filled when baking cakes.
   a If the oven is filled with cakes, the volume of steam given off will be fairly large and will act upon the surfaces of the cakes, keeping them moist.

   b ....

   ....

18 If cakes are placed in a cool oven, aeration proceeds at a good rate, but what effect does this have on the cake?

   ....

   ....

19 When lemon juice is to be added to a cake batter, why is it best to add it after the eggs have been thoroughly mixed in?

   ....

   ....

20 Glycerine is an ingredient which is used in cake mixing; it is known to be hygroscopic. Why use glycerine? What is meant by hygroscopic?

   ....

   ....

   ....

21 Why should rich fruit cakes be stored before being decorated? For how long and in what kind of storage?

   ....

   ....

22 What contamination threats does one have to be aware of when referring to cakes, and how can these threats be minimised?

....

....

....

....

23 Why does the presence of grease destroy the aeration of sponge?

....

....

24 If grease destroys the aeration of sponge batters, an extra light cake can be produced by the addition of melted butter at the time of adding the flour. Why is this?

....

....

25 Why do Swiss rolls sometimes crack when being rolled? Why do chocolate Swiss rolls have a greater tendency to crack?

....

....

26 Why are GMS and other emulsifiers added to commercial Swiss rolls?

....

....

27 A sponge batter containing sugar and 100 per cent fat will take more egg than one which contains sugar and butter or margarine. Explain the effect of water on this.

....

....

28 State the method of producing a sponge using:
The traditional sponge method:

....

....

....

....

An emulsifier:

....

....

....

....

29 State the changes required for correct recipe balance if ground almonds are added to a Swiss roll sheet.

....

....

30 State the approximate percentage by which cornflour can replace flour in a sponge mix. What effect does cornflour have on the mix?

....

....

31 List the types of ingredients which are essential to the success of a high ratio cake mix. How do these ingredients differ from normal types suitable for use in conventional cake mixing?

....

....

....

....

32 Eggs, yeast and chemical raising agents are all used to achieve aeration in baked goods. Explain how the aeration occurs for each and give the conditions necessary for a successful product.

Eggs:

....

....

....

Yeast:

....

....

....

Chemicals:

....

....

....

33 If you are required to use a chocolate sponge pre-mix, how does the production method differ from making a conventional genoise?

....

....

34 Referring to the sponge pre-mix, state the relevance of:

Scaling:

....

....

Baking times:

....

....

Temperatures:

....

....

35 How should the following be stored?
Baking powder:

....

Sheets of baked sponge:

....

36 State the storage problems related to baked goods and general mise-en-place in any establishment or training institution in which you have worked.

....

....

37 How do you think general storage could be improved in relation to any pastry department?

....

....

38 Lucerne fruit and pastry cream roulade is produced from sheets of Swiss roll. Suggest four variations to this recipe and state why this product is suitable for banquets. How should it be stored?

....

....

....

....

....

....

....

....

....

....

39 Give an example of a torten. Using your creativity and imagination, design a torten product. List all the ingredients and describe your produce using a diagram.

40   Give an example of teabread. Suggest a suitable recipe.

....

....

....

....

....

....

....

....

....

41   Name a classic gâteau which may be produced from the ingredients below. Itemise the method of production.

10 whites of egg
200 g (8 oz) ground almonds
25 g (1 oz) cornflour
200 g (8 oz) praline buttercream
50 g (2 oz) chocolate fondant

....

....

....

....

....

....

42 Name three types of sponge or cake product which may be produced from the following methods.

Preparation method	Product
Creaming	Madeira cake ....
Folding	Gâteau Japonnaise ....
Rubbing In	Coconut cake ....
Aeration	Genoise ....
Chemical raising agent	Scones ....

43 Give an example when steam is introduced into the baking process and state its purpose.

....

....

....

....

....

44 Name products which are finished using the following methods.

Finishing methods	Product
Glazing	Fruit meringue torte
Piping	Gâteau mocha
Dusting	Baked cheese cake
Portioning	Apple and raisin roulade

45 What effect does the following have in cakes? Use one or two words for the answer.
Fat insufficiently rubbed in:

....

Too much fat:

....

Too much liquid:

....

Oven too cool:

....

Fruit wet:

....

Too little liquid:

....

Too much baking powder:

....

Oven too hot:

....

Fat to flour ratio incorrect:

....

46 Name two different types of oven suitable for baking.

....

47 List the quality points you would look for in baked goods.

....

....

....

48 State any problems you have observed recently when producing any baked products. List how you will overcome these problems.

....

....

....

....

....

....

....

....

49 List some common faults found in sponges.
Example   Close texture, caused by underbeating of eggs; too much flour; oven too cool or too hot.

....

....

....

....

50 The following are common faults to be found in the production of genoese. State why they could occur.
Close texture:

....

....

....

....

Sunken:

....

....

....

....

Heavy:

....

....

....

....

51 Using a basic 24 cm (10 in) genoese sponge, create a filling and finish which should be suitable for a special occasion. Give a suitable occasion and design the top accordingly.

52 List six afternoon tea pastries which use a sponge or cake mixing.

....

....

....

53 List any trends you have observed in the production of cakes and sponges.
Example Information on different types of ingredients, pre-mixes, etc.

....

....

....

....

54 Discuss ways in which wastage can be minimised when producing sponge and cake products.

....

....

....

55 How should equipment and food surfaces be dealt with in relation to current legislation?

....

....

....

Record of Achievement – Completion of Unit 3F3

Candidate's signature   ....

Assessor's signature   ....

Date   ....

Unit 3F4

Produce pastillage, marzipan, chocolate and sugar products

3F4.1 *Prepare and use pastillage, marzipan and decorative icings*

1   List two recipes for pastillage, one using gum tragacanth, the other using gelatine.

....

....

....

....

....

....

2   Why is cornflour used as an ingredient in pastillage?

....

....

3   Suggest an alternative starch to cornflour.

....

4   How should colour be added to pastillage?

....

....

5 List the specialised equipment you require when working with pastillage.

   ....

   ....

   ....

6 Describe how pastillage should be:
   Rolled:

   ....

   ....

   Cut:

   ....

   ....

7 How does the texture of pastillage affect the overall working quality and performance?

   ....

   ....

8 How is pastillage assembled?

   ....

   ....

9 Pastillage after making should be allowed to rest for 24 hours, completely covered with polythyene or clingfilm in an airtight container to prevent drying out. What are the problems associated with pastillage if used immediately?

   ....

   ....

10 Why are the following working principles essential when using pastillage?
   a The table is spotlessly clean.

   ....

   ....

b The environment is clean.

....

....

c The atmosphere is dry.

....

....

11 The cut pieces of pastillage must be allowed to dry, turning during the drying process. What may the pieces be allowed to dry on?

a Glass

b ....

c ....

d ....

12 Why is the use of food templates so important when working with pastillage?

....

....

13 Suggest an alternative gum to tragacanth that may be used in the production of pastillage.

....

....

14 If during working the pastillage starts to toughen and dry out, how can this be rectified?

....

....

15 Design a display centrepiece to follow a theme of your choice using pastillage. Name the theme and sketch the centrepiece using colour. Describe all the stages needed to make and finish the centrepiece. Finally, describe how you would present and display the finished piece to achieve maximum effect.

16 Give a brief description of the product fondant.

....

....

17 At what temperature should fondant be used?

....

18 As fondant rises in temperature, the sugar crystal gets larger and thus less light can pass through. What effect does this have on the finished product?

....

19 When thinning fondant, it is advisable to use a syrup solution. What is the degree Baumé for the syrup?

....

20 Why add glycerine to royal icing? What effect does the addition of acetic acid have?

....

....

21 Name two ways in which the air may be dispersed from royal icing apart from mixing under vacuum.

....

....

22 What is the name of the machine that mixes under vacuum?

....

23 Name a commercial product suitable for covering sponges and rich fruit cakes to give a decorative finish that may be piped over.

....

24 List the specialised tools now available for enhancing the decorative appearance of soft-moulded icings. Enhance your answer with drawings.

25 American frosting is another type of decorative icing. Name two others.

....

26 What hygiene precautions must be taken into account during the production of boiled buttercream?

....

....

....

27 When finishing a rich fruit cake with royal icing, describe by the use of drawings six decorative edges that may be used. State what number tubes and shapes you would employ.

28 What texture should royal icing be for run-outs?

    ....

29 Good quality wax paper is ideal when making royal icing run-outs. If wax paper is unavailable, what could you use?

    ....

30 Using your creativity and imagination, design a three-tier wedding cake, stating the sizes of each tier. Make maximum use of labelling to describe the design.

31 What special care must be taken when producing run-outs?

a ....

b ....

c ....

d ....

e ....

32 What are the appropriate drying conditions for run-outs and how should they be stored?

....

....

33 Name the two distinct types of almond used in marzipan.

....

34 How is marzipan made commercially?

....

....

....

35 Hard granulated sugar and white of egg is added to the almond paste to produce commercial ....

36 List six products using marzipan.
Example Battenburg

....

....

....

37 What gum solution is used to finish English rout biscuits?

....

38 Describe the production of six marzipan petit fours. Sketch the finishes and any variation in the space provided.

39 List four hygiene principles that have to be taken into account when working with marzipan.

....

....

....

....

40 List any special equipment you would use for specialised marzipan products.

....

....

41 How should marzipan goods be stored?

....

....

42 Describe briefly how you would cover a rich fruit cake with marzipan.

....

....

43 Using the circle, design a marzipan plaque with two marzipan flowers and leaves with an inscription of your choice.

44 *Macaroon recipe*
200 g (8 oz) icing sugar
4 egg whites
vanilla essence
25 g (1 oz) caster sugar for the meringue

What weight of ground almonds is required to make the above recipe workable?

....

3F4.2 *Prepare, process and finish chocolate coatings and couverture-based products*

1 Why should chocolate be treated with great care?

....

....

2 List six items of equipment needed when working with chocolate, and any additional equipment you like to use.
 a Thermometer

 b Double ....

 c Dipping ....

 d ....

 e ....

 f ....

3 Why is cooking chocolate unsuitable for moulding?

....

....

4 How does cooking chocolate or chocolate substitute differ from couverture?

....

....

5 Real chocolate is produced from cocoa beans, roasted and ground to produce a
....

6 Cocoa butter and chocolate liquor forms the basis of all chocolate products; the higher the percentage of cocoa solids contained in the chocolate, the .... the chocolate.

7 How should chocolate be melted?

....

8 The temperature should not go above ....°C (..........°F).

9 Workable consistency of chocolate is around 40 to ....°C (104 to ....°F).

10 How should chocolate be heated in a microwave?

....

....

11 Why is tempering necessary?

....

....

12 When tempering, the chocolate is first allowed to reach ....°C (..........°F), and then cooled to 25 to 27°C (.......... to ....°F). The temperature is then raised to 31 to 32°C (.......... to ....°F).

13 List three points to remember when tempering chocolate.
   a Do not attempt to melt chocolate over direct heat.

   b ....

   c ....

14 Name three ingredients that may be added to chocolate.

....

....

107

15 Describe the making of piping ganache used for decorating and name the ingredients used.

....

....

....

....

16 Give a recipe for hand moulding chocolate.

....

....

17 Many different moulds are now available for use in making confectionery. List the moulds you have recently used and explain what special care has to be taken with the moulds.

....

....

....

18 How should finished chocolate goods be protected?

....

....

19 Outline the procedure for dipping chocolates.

....

....

....

20 Give a recipe for white chocolate truffles. List any variations you are familiar with.

....

....

....

21 Using your imagination and creative flair, design ten finishes for individual chocolates or chocolate pastries.

22 Describe the process of chocolate marbling, using a combination of white and dark chocolate.

....

....

23 When would you use a spray gun on chocolate pieces?

....

24 Packaging chocolates is highly sophisticated for preservation and for psychological reasons. Suggest suitable packaging for chocolates that will both preserve the product and enhance the appearance.

....

....

<u>3F4.3</u> *Process and finish sugar-based products*

1   Sugar is one of the most complicated foods used in food production. It can also be one of the most dangerous. Why?

....

....

2   Sugar is known to be hygroscopic. What does this mean?

....

3   What effect does this have on the handling properties?

....

....

4   State the hygiene precautions to be followed when working with sugar.

....

....

....

....

5   The amount of glucose you add to the sugar and water will vary depending on the effect you wish to achieve. Describe briefly the effects on the finished product if too much glucose has been added to a sugar solution for pulled sugar.

....

....

6   Name an ingredient which could be added to a sugar solution if glucose is unavailable, to obtain a similar type of solution.

....

7   List two non-crystalline sugars.

....

8 What kind of a sugar is honey?

....

9 How should colour be added to boiled sugar?

....

10 What advantages does powder colour have over liquid colour, if any?

....

....

11 List the specialised equipment you are aware of which is used when working with pulled, blown and poured sugar.

....

....

....

12 What are the reasons for using a gas jet?

....

....

13 One reason for adding calcium carbonate to poured sugar is to give an opaque effect. Give another reason.

....

....

14 State the percentage of calcium carbonate required and the temperature at which it is to be added.

....

15 How should completed sugar work be kept?

....

16 Design a centrepiece using poured sugar. The design should suggest a modern theme and be relatively quick and easy to produce.

17 For what purpose are the following used:
Template:

....

Plasticine:

....

Spray gun:

....

Copper boiler:

....

Marble slab:

....

Paper cone:

....

18 State the method for, and two uses of, spun sugar.

....

....

....

19 *Rock sugar recipe*
500 g (1 lb) sugar cubes
200 mls (⅜ pt) water

How much royal icing is required?

....

20 Give two uses of rock sugar.

....

21 What is blown sugar used for?

....

22 Why is it advisable to use an infra-red lamp when working with blown sugar?

....

....

23 What is meant by the word 'sanitised' when applied to sugar cooking?

....

....

24 Describe the process of pulling sugar.

....

....

....

....

25 Why would you use a heat gun?

....

....

26 Why might fruits weep after being dipped in boiling sugar?

....

....

27 Describe in simple terms the chemical change which takes place when boiling sugar.

....

....

28 Describe the method of making caramel.

....

....

....

29 Complete the following sugar table:

Stage of sugar boiling	Description	Uses	Temperature
Small thread		Stock syrup	104°C ... °F
Large thread	Threads are more numerous and stronger		110°C ... °F
Soft ball	Sugar forms a soft ball	Fondant	116°C ... °F
Hard ball		Sweets Petits fours	121°C ... °F
Small crack		Meringue	... °C ... °F
Large crack		Dipping fruits	153°C ... °F
Caramel			... °C ... °F

For many pastry dishes, such as ice-cream and sorbets, sugar syrups of a definite density are required.

30 What is meant by density?

....

....

31 How is density measured?

....

....

32 What is a saccharometer?

....

....

33 At what density should the syrup be for sorbet? (Give your answer in degrees Baumé.)

....

34 Why is this knowledge of syrup density important for the pastry department?

....

....

35 State why the density of syrup has to be correct when poaching different types of fruit.

....

....

36 How does the density of syrup differ with the ripeness of the fruit?

....

....

37 Complete the following table.

Sugar dissolved in 250 ml (1 pt) water		Reading on Baumé saccharometer at 30°C (60°F)
g	oz	
50	2	5°
100	4	. . . .
150	6	12°
200	8	15°
250	10	18°
300	12	. . . .
350	14	23°
400	16	24.5°
450	18	. . . .
500	20	28°
550	22	. . . .
600	24	30°

Record of Achievement – Completion of Unit 3F4

Candidate's signature ....

Assessor's signature ....

Date ....

KITCHEN AND LARDER WORK

Prepare and cook complex fish and shellfish dishes

3F5.1 *Prepare complex fish dishes*

The supply of fresh fish varies throughout the year according to when fish are in season. Quality will also vary owing to factors such as breeding and spawning periods. It is essential to have a good working relationship with the fish suppliers and/or the fish market, to be fully aware of what is the best fish of suitable quality and acceptable price. The farming of certain fish – salmon, trout, turbot and sea bass, for example – has been studied and developed for many years, and has had the effect of creating a great supply of fish on the market at certain times of the year.

1 Complete the following quality points relating to wet fish and frozen fish.

> Eyes: bright, full and not sunken, no slime or cloudiness.
>
> Gills: ....
>
> ....
>
> Flesh: firm and resilient so that when pressed the impression goes quickly.
>
> Scales: ....
>
> ....
>
> Skin: should be covered with fresh sea slime or be smooth, and must have a good skin and no abrasions.
>
> Frozen fish:...
>
> ....

2 Why is the purchasing unit of fish important in relation to portion control and ways of minimising waste?

....

....

3 An average weight per portion for fish would be?
Off the bone:

....

On the bone:

....

4 When purchasing large fish on the bone, such as turbot, how much weight should be allowed per portion?

....

5 A 3½ kg (7 lb) turbot will yield approximately how many portions?

....

6 When specific cuts of fish at a certain weight are required, why is it important to ensure that an economic size of fish is ordered? For example, if a party for 200 is to be served with darnes of salmon, what could be the effect of ordering 120 lb of whole salmon?

....

....

....

7 What are the main contamination threats when storing and preparing fish dishes and how can the risks be minimised?

....

....

....

8 How should the following fish be stored and at what temperature?
Fresh fish:

....

Frozen fish:

....

Smoked fish:

....

9 Name four popular fish in each category and describe their characteristics.
Flat fish:

....

....

Round fish:

....

....

Smoked fish:

....

....

10 What is the nutritional value of the various types of fish?

....

....

....

11 After the fish has been prepared and before it is cooked, it must be kept in a refrigerator. What is the minimum temperature at which the refrigerator should be set and for how long can it safely be held at this temperature?

....

....

12 List seven rules for the correct use of knives:

   a Use the correct knife for the appropriate job.

   b ....

   c ....

   d ....

   e ....

   f ....

   g Do not put knives into a sink of washing-up water.

13 What is the danger of a fish bone breaking the skin on the hand and what is the treatment?

....

....

....

....

14 Why is personal hygiene so important in relation to food? Outline the reasons in full.

....

....

....

....

15 What are the dangers of cross-contamination when handling fresh fish?

....

....

16 How should the waste from fish preparation be disposed of?

....

17 Flies are attracted to fish. What is the danger of flies landing on fish and how can flies be controlled?

....

....

18 What are the penalties that can result from being found guilty of an offence under the Food Safety Act?

....

....

19 Write out a hygiene check list for the fish preparation area.

....

....

....

....

20 What is the difference in removing the black skin from a lemon and a Dover sole?

....

21 What are the four stages of preparing a whole turbot for cutting into slices on the bone?

....

....

....

....

22 When filleting a whole turbot, is it necessary to first remove the head and side fins?

....

23 What are the four stages of preparing a whole uncleaned salmon?

....

....

....

....

24 When round fish are cooked whole, why are they sometimes scored?

....

25 What is the difference in preparing for grilling between herring and mackerel?

....

....

26 Describe the preparation of the following cuts of fish and name a suitable fish in each case.
    Tronçon:

....

....

    Darne:

....

....

    Plait:

....

....

Goujon/goujonette:

....

....

Fillet:

....

....

Délice:

....

....

Suprême:

....

....

Paupiette:

....

....

27 Describe the preparation of a suitable fish to be cooked whole and one to be stuffed and cooked whole.

....

....

....

....

28 The following are all methods of raw fish preparation – in each case name a suitable fish and describe the method.
Mincing/processing:

....

....

Portioning:

....

....

Carving:

....

....

Stuffing:

....

....

Trussing/tying:

....

....

Marinating:

....

....

Filleting:

....

....

Descaling:

....

....

Skinning:

....

....

Coating:

....

....

Reforming/moulding:

....

....

Batting:

....

....

29 Describe the preparation of a salmon coulibiac.

....

....

....

....

30 Mousse, mousseline and quenelles are made from the same basic mixture. State the ingredients and proportions for a fish farce.

....

....

31 When making a fish farce, why is it necessary for the mixture to be ice-cold when beating in the cream?

....

....

32 When half of the cream is added, how can the mixture be tested before adding further cream?

....

....

33 Give two reasons for testing the mixture.

....

....

34 When preparing a fish mousse for four portions, why is it wiser to prepare four individual moulds rather than one large one?

....

35 Name two ways in which fish mousse can be cooked.

....

....

36 Describe the method of shaping:
Mousselines:

....

Quenelles:

....

37 Describe the preparation for the cooking of:
Eels:

....

Squid:

....

38 Why is red mullet sometimes referred to as woodcock of the sea? How does this affect the cleaning and preparation of red mullet?

....

....

39 When preparing paupiettes, name the three ways in which they can be kept in shape:
a Tying with fine string.

b ....

c ....

40 Name and describe two suitable fillings for paupiettes of sole.

....

....

41 Name and describe two suitable fillings for sardines.

....

....

42 Name three other fish that can be prepared in this way.

....

43 Name four suitable additions to a fish farce for stuffing a turbot.

....

....

44 Is it possible to remove the black skin of turbot or brill while raw? Explain your answer.

....

....

....

3F5.2 *Cook and finish complex fish dishes*

Among current trends in fish cookery are an ever-increasing popularity in fish dishes, sauces of a very light consistency and the influence of Asian and Eastern cookery.

1   Discuss any other trends of which you are aware.

   ....

   ....

   ....

2   What are the main contamination threats when cooking and storing fish and how can these be minimised?

   ....

   ....

   ....

The nutritional value of fish is as useful as that of meat and is preferred by many people in place of meat.

3   How during cooking can the maximum nutritional value be retained?
   a   Do not overcook.

   b   With shallow poached fish, always use the cooking liquor in the coating sauce.

   c   ....

   d   ....

4   Fish is as useful as a source of animal protein as meat.   True/False

5   Poached or steamed fish can be ½ to ¾ cooked, as the cooking will complete during the holding process. Discuss this statement in relation to large-scale cookery.

   ....

   ....

   ....

6 Fish can be grilled either on open bars or under a salamander. When grilling over heat on open bars, what previous preparation is required to the grill bars before cooking and why?

....

....

7 Name four fish suitable for grilling on open bars and suggest ways in which additional flavour(s) can be added to each dish or as an accompaniment.

a Grilled sea bass with fennel.

b ....

c ....

d ....

8 Fish can be grilled under the salamander in two ways:
a Between a well-oiled, centre-hinged double wire grid with a handle.

b On a ....

9 Name two fish suitable for cooking by either method and suggest a suitable accompanying sauce or/and accompaniments in each case.

....

....

10 How would you grill sardines approximately 16 cm (6 in) in length?

....

....

11 When grilling a sea bass, how could the flavour of fennel be injected?

....

....

12 Name four fish that can be cooked by deep poaching.

....

....

13 State whether these can be cooked whole or in a named cut.

....

....

14 Give a recipe for the cooking liquor in each case.

....

....

....

....

15 Suggest a sauce that could accompany each choice.

....

....

16 After being cooked by deep poaching, what should be done to slices of fish on the bone before serving?

   Cod and salmon: ....

   Turbot and brill:...

17 If serving an egg-and-butter-based sauce, why should it be offered separately rather than masked over the fish? Give two reasons.

....

....

18 Give two reasons why a hollandaise sauce may curdle.

....

....

19 State two ways in which a curdled hollandaise sauce can be reconstituted.

....

....

20 To reduce the risk of salmonella infection when using egg-based sauces, what are two measures that can be taken?

....

....

21 If you are required to produce tronçons of turbot and you are to be supplied with one 10 kg (20 lb) turbot, what action would you take?

....

....

22 When deep poaching a whole salmon for the cold buffet:
  a Should the fish be placed into hot or cold liquid?

....

  b What is the name of the cooking liquid used?

....

  c Should the salmon be removed when hot or left in the liquid to go cold?

....

  d Give an approximate cooking time for a 3½ kg (7 lb) salmon and a 14 kg (28 lb) salmon.

....

23 What are the traditional accompaniments to a hot darne of salmon?

....

....

24 List six advantages to cooking fish by steaming.
   a Retention of nutritional value.

   b ....

   c ....

   d ....

   e ....

   f Suitable for large-scale cookery.

25 What is the name given to the process of steaming food in vacuum-sealed plastic pouches?

....

26 List six advantages to this method of cooking.
   a Minimal change of texture and weight loss.

   b ....

   c ....

   d ....

   e ....

   f Uniformity of standard.

27 Describe the preparation and cooking of a dish of fish fillets with mushrooms, herbs and white wine using the above method.

....

....

....

....

28 Once vacuum pouches are cooked they must be quickly .... and kept at a temperature of ....°.

29 How are vacuum pouches then re-heated for service?

....

....

30 Outline the general method for shallow poaching fish.
   a Butter the cooking pan.

   b Ensure the fish is correctly prepared and cleaned.

   What is meant by correctly prepared in the case of:
      Fish fillets:

....

      Whole fish, e.g. slip soles:

....

   c If using chopped shallots as a base ensure that they are ....
      .... and ....

   d ....

   e ....

   f ....

   g Poach .... in .... or ....

   h ....

   i ....

   j ....

   k ....

31 What principles should be observed when poaching fish to retain maximum flavour and nutritive value?

....

....

32 After being cooked, what should be done to poached fish before coating with sauce?

....

....

33 Name six fish suitable for shallow poaching, giving a garnish and sauce suitable for each and naming each dish as it would appear on a menu.

....

....

....

....

....

....

34 If using tomato and grapes in a poached fish dish, name two ways in which they should be prepared?

....

....

35 Suggest four foods suitable for use as the base for a poached fish dish.

a Mushroom purée

b ....

c ....

d ....

A classic fish sauce is made by reducing the strained fish cooking liquor to a light glaze then mounting with butter and possibly adding lightly whipped cream.

36 Outline other methods of making a fish sauce and explain how a fish sauce for 500 guests would be produced.

....

....

....

....

37 Name the vaious cuts of fish suitable for shallow poaching and give the name of the fish from which they are prepared in each case.

....

....

....

....

Certain fish are suitable for braising either whole, e.g. sea bass, bream and salmon; in large pieces, e.g. tuna and salmon; or in thick slices on the bone, e.g. salmon. Smaller fish cuts can also be cooked by a simple form of braising. Whole fish may be stuffed if required.

38 Give three recipes of your choice, one for a whole fish, one for a 2 kg (4 lb) piece and one for 6 × 200 g (8 oz) slices on the bone.

a ....

....

....

....

b ....

....

....

....

c ....

....

....

....

39 What is the essential requirement of a fat or oil to be used for fat frying?

....

40 What is meant by the smoke point and the flash point?

....

....

41 Why are temperature and time control so important in relation to deep-fried foods, particularly when quantities of food are being continuously fried?

....

....

42 What is the danger of deep frying in a fryer that is overfull of fat or oil?

....

43 What is the danger of placing food that has not been properly dried into hot deep fat?

....

44 A normal frying temperature is between 175–195°C (350–380°F). If the thermometer fails, how can this degree of heat be indicated?

....

45 What happens to the food if the frying is loaded with too much fat at one time?

....

46 Why is it important to strain the deep frying oil or fat after each use?

....

47 When a fryer is not in use, how can oxidation be prevented?

....

48 What is the danger of oxidation of deep fat?

....

49 What should you do before straining the oil or fat of a fryer?

....

....

50 What procedure should be followed if a deep fat fryer ignites?

....

....

51 Why should water never be used on fat fires?

....

52 Which fire extinguishers should be at hand for deep fat fryers?

....

53 When should the fat or oil in a fryer be discarded and why?

....

....

54 What are the characteristics of a good frying batter?

....

....

55 What is the purpose of coating fish before deep frying?

....

56 Name three ways of coating fish before deep frying.

....

....

....

57 Suggest three different sauces suitable for serving with fried fish.

....

....

....

58 Fish fried orly style is first marinated in oil, lemon juice and parsley. Suggest three other types of marinades suitable for fish.

....

....

....

59 State the procedure for frying whitebait.

....

....

60 Name four fish suitable for frying whole or in fillets or cuts. Suggest a suitable accompanying sauce and/or garnish in each case.

....

....

....

....

61 Give the basic principles of shallow frying to ensure a first-class product.

....

....

....

62 What is the difference between shallow-fried fish and fish meunière?

....

....

63 Suggest four different fish that can be shallow-fried whole, and four fish each in a different cut. Which garnish(es) would you use and how would they appear on a menu?

....

....

....

....

64 If a slice or slices of lemon are placed on shallow-fried fish, how should the lemon slices be prepared and why?

....

....

65 Outline the basic principles for stir-fry fish dishes.

....

....

....

....

66 Give the recipes for two interesting stir-fry fish dishes, including a marinade and sauce in each case.

a ....

....

....

....

....

....

b ....

....

....

....

....

....

Many fish dishes can be prepared by stewing, e.g. eels and bouillabaisse which is a famous French dish. After studying this recipe it is obvious that there can be many variations produced depending on the types of fish available.

67 Using your own ideas, produce two recipes for fish stews.

a ....

....

....

....

....

b ....

....

....

....

....

68 Suggest two whole fish and two cuts of fish suitable for baking and, using your own ideas, give a recipe and method for one of each.

a ....

....

....

....

....

b ....

....

....

....

....

Fish murat is a popular classic dish cooked by sautéeing.

69 Using your own ideas, produce two fish recipes cooked by sautéeing.

a ....

....

....

....

....

b ....

....

....

....

....

70 Name and give a brief description of two dishes for each of the following:
Farce:

....

....

....

....

Mousseline:

....

....

....

....

Quenelles:

....

....

....

....

3F5.3 *Prepare complex shellfish dishes*

To ensure freshness, whenever possible all shellfish should be purchased live.

1 What are the possible exceptions to this rule?

....

....

2 How are the following tested to see that they are live?
Oysters, mussels, clams, scallops (bivalves):

....

Lobsters, crabs, scampi, prawns:

....

3 If frozen shellfish have to be purchased, what are the quality points that should be looked for?

....

....

4 If scallops are bought out of the shell, how is the freshness and quality assessed?

....

....

5 When determining quality in lobsters and crabs, why is it important to relate the size to the weight of the fish?

....

....

6 What is the main nutritional value of shellfish?

....

7   What are the main contamination threats when preparing and storing shellfish and how should they be avoided?

....

....

....

8   When buying crabs, why is it important to see that there are two good-sized claws.

....

9   What is the approximate cooking time for a 2½ kg (5 lb) crab?

....

10 When preparing crab, what are the two parts that should be removed and discarded?

....

11 What should be the consistency of the brown meat of crab?

....

12 After all the white meat has been removed from the crab, why is it best to use the fingers for shredding it?

....

13 When cutting up live lobsters, what are the two parts that should be removed and discarded?

....

14 If the dish for which the lobster is to be used requires a lobster sauce, what is the advantage of having hen lobsters?

....

15 How can the hen lobster be identified when live? Make a comparison with the cock lobster.

....

....

16 When preparing cooked lobster, why is it important that the trail (intestinal tract) not only be removed but also washed if necessary?

....

....

17 What would be the effect on the lobster meat in the tails and claws if they are over-boiled?

....

18 How would lobster meat be cut for the following?
  Cocktail bouchées:

....

  Lobster Mornay:

....

19 How are cooked shrimps prepared?

....

20 How are the tails from live prawns prepared for cooking?

....

21 What is the preparation before and after cooking of Dublin Bay prawns and crayfish?

....

....

22 What is essential in the preparation of cockles before cooking and why is this so?

....

....

23 What two things must you do to prepare mussels for cooking?

  a Scrape the shells to remove ....

  b ....

24 Why, after being cooked, does each mussel need to be opened and checked? What could be the effect of this not being done?

....

....

25 Describe the opening and cleaning of live scallops.

....

....

26 What is the orange curved portion attached to some scallops and can this be used?

....

27 What are the signs of freshness in clams?

....

....

28 As clams live in sand, how should this be ejected?

....

29 Why should the shells of oysters be tightly shut?

....

30 Why should a proper oyster knife be used to open oysters? What other precaution is required to protect the hand?

....

31 What is the danger if opened oysters are roughly cut from their shells?

....

32 Should oysters be washed before being placed in the deep half-shell and, if so, why?

....

33 Where and how should live oysters be kept after delivery?

....

....

34 Outline the preparation for:
Fish farce:

....

....

Lobster mousse (using live lobster) to be served hot:

....

....

Mousselines of lobster:

....

....

Quenelles of lobster for a fish dish garnish:

....

....

3F5.4 *Cook and finish complex shellfish dishes*

1 Using your own ideas, suggest two ways in which crab can be served cold and two ways it can be served as a hot dish.

....

....

....

....

2 What are two ways in which hot lobster soufflé can be served?

....

....

3 For the following, discuss which of the two methods you would adopt and give your reasons why.

A small number of portions, à la carte service:

....

Large parties of 100–500 persons:

....

4 When cooking a hot lobster dish to be served in the half-shell, e.g. lobster Mornay, what are the important points to observe and what are the points that can lead to a poor quality dish?

....

....

....

5 Using your own ideas, suggest six ways of serving lobster, three cold and three hot.

....

....

....

....

....

....

6 When and why is it necessary to tie the tail of a live crawfish to a piece of wood before cooking?

....

7 Suggest two recipes for a hot dish of crawfish, and two recipes for a cold dish.

....

....

....

....

8 Suggest interesting ways of preparing and serving shrimps:
As a hot cocktail canapé:

....

As an egg dish:

....

As a hot fish dish:

....

As part of a garnish for a hot fish dish:

....

As a hot savoury:

....

Could prawns also be used for any of the above dishes?

9 Suggest three other hot dishes using prawns as the main ingredient.

....

....

10 Describe three dishes for each of the following:
Dublin Bay prawns:

....

....

....

Crayfish:

....

....

....

11 Suggest four dishes, two hot and two cold, using cockles.

....

....

12 Outline the method for making a risotto with cockles.

....

....

13 Suggest four interesting ways for serving mussels hot.

....

....

14 Why is it important to cook scallops for the minimum possible time?

....

15 Using your own ideas, suggest three ways in which scallops can be cooked and served hot in their shells and three ways out of the shells.

....

....

....

....

....

16 Describe two hot dishes in which scallops can be used in combination with other foods.

....

....

17 Outline the method of making, cooking and serving a hot scallop mousse with a suitable sauce.

....

....

18 Suggest a recipe for serving clams:
Au gratin:

....

As a stir-fry dish:

....

19 When oysters are opened and served cold on the half-shell, the natural juice is served in the deep shell. Why is this done?

....

20 What should happen to the natural juices when oysters are being cooked?

....

21 If it is to be cooked, for how long should an oyster be poached?

....

22 Name four interesting dishes of hot oysters, two for a cocktail reception and two for a fish course.

....

....

....

....

23 Suggest a dish of hot shellfish quenelles. Outline the method of cooking and serving and name a suitable sauce.

....

....

....

....

24 Describe two complex fish dishes which you have prepared or seen in your establishment, and outline the preparation and serving for:
    Plate service:

....

....

    Silver service:

....

....

25 If suitable for a banquet, list the ingredients for 100 portions.

....

....

....

....

....

....

Record of Achievement – Completion of Unit 3F5

Candidate's signature   ....

Assessor's signature   ....

Date   ....

Unit 3F6

Prepare and cook complex meat, offal, game and poultry dishes

3F6.1 *Prepare complex meat and offal dishes*

1 Outline the points of quality in the following:

Liver:

....

....

   Kidneys:

....

....

   Hearts:

....

....

   Tongue:

....

....

   Sweetbreads:

....

....

2 What are the points of quality relating to:
Frozen meat:

....

....

Chilled meat:

....

....

Fresh meat:

....

....

3 Name the joints on the following diagrams and list the various cuts that are obtained from them.
Lamb:

1 ....
2 ....
3 ....
4 ....
5 ....
6 ....
7 ....

Beef hindquarter:

1 ....
2 ....
3 ....
4 ....
5 ....
6 ....
7 ....
8 ....
9 ....
9A ....

Veal:

1 ....
2 ....
3 ....
4 ....
5 ....
6 ....
7 ....
8 ....

Leg of veal:

1 ....
2 ....
3 ....
4 ....
5 ....

Pork:

1 ....
2 ....
3 ....
4 ....
5 ....
6 ....

Bacon:

1 ....
2 ....
3 ....
4 ....
5 ....

4 What are the main contamination threats when preparing and storing raw meat and offal dishes and how can the risks be minimised?

....

....

....

5 The nutritional value of meat is in having a high .... content which is valuable for the .... and .... of the body and as a source of ....

6 The two extra elements contained in liver are vitamin .... and ....

7 Sweetbreads are particularly valuable for hospital diets because they are easily .... and are useful for building body ....

8 Why must fresh meat be allowed to hang before being used?

....

9 What is the effect on meat after being correctly hung?

....

10 What is the usual temperature for hanging meat?

....

11 The ideal storage temperature for fresh meat is .... at a relative humidity of .... per cent.

12 Under proper hygienic conditions at these temperatures, safe storage times are:

    Beef: up to .... weeks.

    Veal: 1 to .... weeks.

    Lamb: 10 to .... days.

    Pork: 7 to .... days.

    Offal: up to .... days.

13 Summarise the health and safety legislation in relation to meat and offal preparation.

....

....

....

14 List the relevant food hygiene regulations relating to meat and offal preparation.

....

....

....

15 Name the four signs of quality in a carcass of lamb.

....

....

16 Briefly describe:
Loin chop:

....

Chump chop:

....

Barnsley chop:

....

17 What is the difference between a short saddle and a full saddle of lamb?

....

18 Briefly describe the preparation of a full saddle of lamb for roasting.

....

....

19 Name two lamb joints suitable for stuffing.

a ....

b ....

20 What are the signs of quality in a correctly prepared best end of lamb and by what other name is a best-end of lamb known?

....

....

21 Describe the preparation of lamb kidneys for:
Grilling:

....

Sauté:

....

22 Should lamb cutlets be batted out before being egg and crumbed? Give reasons for your answer.

....

....

23 Suggest four different additions that can be made to the breadcrumbs for crumbing lamb cutlets.

....

....

....

....

24 Is there any point other than tradition in preparing noisettes and rosettes of lamb in different shapes? Give reasons for your answer.

....

....

25 Give two reasons why, when preparing a saddle of lamb, it should be scored?

....

....

26 What are the characteristics of good-quality beef?

....

....

27 Describe the preparation of sirloin of beef for roasting:
On the bone:

....

Off the bone:

....

28 Briefly describe the preparation and give an average weight for:
Sirloin steak:

....

Minute steak:

....

Porterhouse steak:

....

T-bone steak:

....

29 How is fillet of beef prepared for cutting into steaks?

....

30 Give a breakdown of the uses and approximate weights of a 3 kg (7 lb) fillet of beef.

....

....

31 How can moisture and flavour be injected into a 600 g (1½ lb) piece of beef fillet for roasting?

....

32 Outline the preparation of a wing rib of beef to be roasted on the bone.

....

....

33 What are the characteristics of good quality veal?

....

....

34 State the procedure for boning a 20 kg (40 lb) leg of veal and the methods of producing escalopes and osso buco.

....

....

....

35 What is the preparation for:
Veal kidneys:

....

Veal sweetbreads:

....

Calves' liver:

....

36 What are the signs of quality in pork?

....

....

37 Describe the preparation of a leg and a loin of pork for roasting.

....

....

38 What are the signs of quality of a side of bacon?

....

....

39 What preparation is required to a side of bacon before it can be cut into rashers?

....

....

40 Are streaky, back and gammon rashers normally always cut thin? Give reasons for your answer.

....

....

41 Is it necessary to pre-soak bacon joints for boiling? Give reasons for your answer.

....

....

42 What is the difference between a gammon and a ham?

....

43 To carve a ham on the bone efficiently, is it necessary to remove the aitch-bone before or after being cooked? Explain your answer.

....

....

44 If a ham is boned out before being boiled, it must be tied before cooking and can be put into a ham press when cooked.   True/False

45 State the preparation required for the following:
   Ox tongue:

....

   Lamb hearts:

....

Tripe:

....

Oxtail:

....

46 Give an example for each of the following methods of preparation:

Brining: ....

Marinading: ....

Batting: ....

Barding: ....

Larding: ....

Stuffing: ....

Rolling: ....

Moulding: ....

47 Which meats would you consider most suitable for making into mousselines and quenelles?

....

....

48 Which meat is most used for forcemeat, farce, pies, pâtés and terrines?

....

49 Describe a modern meat dish which you have experienced which uses offal as a garnish. The dish should be suitable for plate service.

....

....

50 State what hygiene precautions have to be taken into account when preparing this dish.

....

3F6.2 *Cook and finish complex meat and offal dishes*

1   Name two prime roasting joints from:

Hindquarter of beef: ....

....

Carcass of lamb: ....

....

Side of veal: ....

....

Side of pork: ....

....

2   From each of the above, name two prime cuts suitable for shallow frying or grilling.

....

....

3   From each of the above, name one joint suitable for braising.

....

....

4   From each of the above, name two joints that can be cut up and used for a stew.

....

....

5   From each of the above, name one cut suitable for stir-frying.

....

....

6   What are the degrees of cooking grilled meats and how can these be tested?

....

7   To test the degree to which offal has been cooked, use pressure to release juice from

the offal. If the offal is required well done no .... will be evident. If

the offal is required pink, then the issuing juice will be .... in colour.

8   Briefly discuss the effects of various cooking methods on meat and offal, the chemical changes and how to maximise and retain maximum nutritional value during cooking.

....

....

9   What are the main contamination threats when cooking and storing meat and offal and how can risks be minimised?

....

....

....

....

10   List the quality points you would use to assess the following dishes cooked and presented ready for service:
   Mixed grill:

....

....

   Lamb cutlets Reform:

....

....

   Navarin of lamb:

....

....

   Kidney sauté:

....

....

Rack of lamb with herbs and garlic:

....

....

Roast stuffed saddle of lamb:

....

....

Fillet of beef Wellington:

....

....

Pepper steak:

....

....

Beef goulash:

....

....

Beef carbonnade:

....

....

Stewed oxtail:

....

....

Braised beef:

....

....

Sauté of veal marengo:

....

....

Veal chop in a paper bag:

....

....

Veal kidneys in mustard sauce:

....

....

Fricassée of veal:

....

....

Escalope of veal viennoise:

....

....

Calf's liver and bacon:

....

....

Roast leg of pork:

....

....

Pork escalopes with prunes:

....

....

Sauté of pork with leeks:

....

....

Barbecue spare ribs:

....

....

Sweet and sour pork:

....

....

Current hygiene regulations require that cooking areas and equipment are kept clean and fully maintained throughout production periods.

11 Discuss this in relation to your own experience and give examples of any bad practices you have observed and how you would rectify them.

....

....

....

....

12 If a customer expresses specific requirements when ordering a meal, how would you ensure that appropriate adjustments are made to the recipe, e.g. the customer may wish to order a specific dish but may have an allergy to one or two ingredients in it? Give examples of two dishes and state the action you would take.

....

....

....

....

13 Name the essential points that ensure the nutritional value of meat and offal is adequately retained during cooking.

....

....

14 How can you ensure that cooking and finishing methods and appropriate recipe adjustments maximise the quality of the dish?

....

....

15 How do you ensure that cooked meat and offal dishes fully meet recipe specifications? Discuss fully.

....

....

....

16 How should cooked meat and offal dishes not required for immediate consumption be stored?

....

17 Outline the correct procedure for roasting a wing rib of beef and for preparing gravy and Yorkshire pudding.

....

....

18 Compare the cooking times per lb of roast beef sirloin and boiled silverside.

....

19 A 1 kg (2 lb) fillet of beef roasted. Outline the method of cooking, the accompanying gravy/sauce and garnish of your choice.

....

....

20 The classical repertoire offers numerous ways of garnishing tournedos. Using your own ideas, suggest three recipes using tournedos.

....

....

....

21 Outline the procedure for preparing and cooking beef Wellington:
Using a 1 kg (2 lb) piece of fillet:

....

As individual portions:

....

22 Considering the procedure for beef Wellington, what variations could you suggest on the basic recipe?

....

23 Recipes for pepper steak vary considerably from establishment to establishment. Suggest a recipe of your own.

....

24 Describe the way in which you think a beef grill should be cooked and served.

....

....

25 Discuss the difference between a *sauté of beef* and a *ragoût of beef*. Give an example of each using your own ideas for a recipe.

....

....

....

26 A steak and kidney pie is popular at any level of catering. Give your recipe for a top quality steak and kidney pie.

....

....

....

27 Give a recipe of your own choice using oxtail.

....

....

....

28 Describe the cooking of an ox tongue.

....

....

29 Describe a hot dish using ox tongue.

....

....

30 Give two recipes illustrating the use of tripe.

....

....

....

31 Give your ideas on producing a rack of lamb with herbs.

....

....

32 There are two recipes for breadcrumbed lamb cutlets in *Advanced Practical Cookery*. Suggest variations or alternatives to each.

....

....

....

33 How would you cook, carve and present an à la carte order for roast saddle of lamb for four people? If required, what garnish would you use?

....

....

....

34 Compare the cooking time per lb of:

Roast leg of lamb: ....

Boiled leg of mutton: ....

35 Give your recipe for shish kebab and describe how you would cook and serve it.

....

....

....

36 Which chops would you select for Champvallon and why?

....

37 Using your own ideas give two recipes for noisettes of lamb.

....

....

....

38 If required to produce a top-quality navarin, what would be your choice of meat and why?

....

39 There are many variations to a hot-pot. Give your idea of a tasty recipe.

....

....

....

40 Unless specifically requested, to what degree would you cook grilled lambs' kidneys?

....

41 How would you prepare and cook devilled kidneys?

....

....

42 Suggest a recipe for a kidney sauté.

....

....

....

43 Give a recipe using sheep's hearts.

....

....

....

44 Using your own ideas, give one recipe each for:
White veal stew:

....

....

Brown veal stew:

....

....

45 Give a recipe of your own choice for:
Breadcrumbed veal escalope:

....

....

Veal escalope:

....

....

46 When cooking a dish of veal escalopes using a wine to flavour the sauce, when and how should the wine be added? Describe in detail how the final sauce is made.

....

....

47 Suggest three wines suitable for addition to a brown dish of veal and three wines suitable for addition to a white dish of veal.

....

....

48 What is the approximate cooking time per lb for a roast leg of veal? How can extra flavour be injected into the dish? How is the gravy prepared? What two accompaniments may be served?

....

....

....

....

49 What are the differences in the cooking techniques for:
Veal escalope viennoise:

....

Veal escalope cordon bleu:

....

50 Suggest two accompaniments for pojarski of veal.

....

51 Outline a recipe of your own choice for osso buco together with accompaniments.

....

....

....

52 Outline the method of producing a veal chop en papillote.

....

....

....

53 State your recipe and method for a dish of veal kidneys with mustard sauce.

....

....

....

54 Give the important points required to cook a top quality dish of:
Calves' liver and bacon:

....

Calves' liver with butter and sage:

....

55 Give a detailed description for the preparation of a dish of veal sweetbreads:
Cooked white:

....

Cooked brown:

....

56 Suggest two recipes with suitable garnish for:
Breadcrumbed sweetbread escalopes:

....

Sweetbread escalopes (uncrumbed):

....

57 Give your ideas for a dish combining sweetbreads and kidneys.

....

....

58 What is the approximate cooking time per lb for roast leg of pork?

....

59 Describe in detail the roasting process, making gravy, apple sauce, dressing (stuffing) carving and serving for:
Four portions:

....

....

....

400 portions:

....

....

....

60 Suggest three recipes of your choice for serving pork chops.

....

....

....

61 Using your own ideas, give a recipe for barbecued pork spare ribs.

....

....

62 Give two recipes using pork escalopes.

....

....

....

63 Outline the technique for cooking and serving a top-quality sausage toad in the hole.

....

....

....

64 Give a recipe of your choice for sweet and sour pork.

....

....

65 Give a detailed description of the cooking and serving of roast suckling pig.

....

....

....

66 Suggest a method of preparing and cooking fillet of pork in pastry with an accompanying sauce.

....

....

67 What is the approximate cooking time per lb for boiled ham or bacon?

....

68 Outline a method of cooking and serving a bacon joint with pineapple.

....

....

69 Suggest two ways of cooking gammon rashers.

....

70 Write as they would appear on a menu two dishes cooked by:

Braising: ....

Roasting: ....

Pot roasting: ....

Stewing: ....

Grilling: ....

Shallow frying: ....

Stir-frying: ....

Sautéeing: ....

Baking: ....

Deep frying: ....

Hot smoking: ....

Poaching/boiling: ....

En papillote: ....

3F6.3 *Prepare complex game and offal dishes*

1   Why is the hanging of game essential? What bird is the exception?

....

2   What would be the effects on the flesh of game if it were not hung? Do young birds need less hanging time than old birds?

....

....

3   List the four factors that determine the hanging time.

....

....

....

....

4   Are game birds plucked or drawn before hanging? Explain your answer.

....

....

5   Which of the following is more suitable for hanging game: a well-ventilated, dry, cold store room not refrigerated or a refrigerator?

....

6   Which of the following is correct?
     Game birds should be hung by the feet with the neck down.
     Game birds should be hung by the neck with the feet down.

7   Name the two quality points for joints of fresh venison.

....

....

8   How can rabbits be distinguished from hares? Name three points.

....

....

....

9   How can the age (old or young) of rabbits and hares be tested?

....

10   What happens to the lip of a hare as it ages?

....

11   How is quality assessed in chilled furred game?

....

12   List the five quality points for feathered game.

Beak: ....

Breast plumage: ....

Breast: ....

Quill feathers: ....

Legs:..

13   How would you ensure portion control and minimise waste when handling game? Explain fully.

....

....

....

....

14 What are the main contamination threats when preparing and storing game and how can the risks be minimised?

....

....

....

....

15 As game is less fatty than meat or poultry, it is easily digested. What is the exception? Explain why.

....

16 Game is also useful for building and repairing ....

and for ....

17 Discuss the storage/holding requirements for prepared uncooked game.

....

....

18 How is the quality of prepared game assessed?

....

....

19 How can you keep up to date with seasonal variations in price, availability and quality of game?

....

....

20 What is the relevant legislation with regard to:
Preparation, storage and hanging of game:

....

Health and safety:

....

Food hygiene:

....

Grouse is probably the most famous and popular game bird.

21 When is grouse in season?

....

22 What is the name sometimes given to the opening day?

....

23 What is an average weight for a grouse?

....

24 How can young grouse be distinguished?

....

25 If grouse are to be prepared and cooked on the day they are shot, what is an essential requirement for them?

....

26 Which would have more flavour, a freshly killed grouse or one that has hung for 5–7 days? Why?

....

After game birds have been sufficiently hung they are feathered (plucked). The feathers must be removed quickly but carefully, otherwise the skins of the birds will be damaged. After feathering/plucking, birds must be checked to ensure that no pens (the ends of feathers) remain in the skin. They are then drawn (eviscerated) as for chickens and the livers are retained for use as game farce. After trussing, a thin bard should be tied over the breast to prevent it drying during cooking.

27 This is standard procedure for all game birds with the exception of woodcock and snipe. Why is this and how are these two birds prepared for roasting?

....

....

28   After grouse, what are the two most popular game birds?

....

29   Given ideal storage conditions, for how long can a carcass of venison be hung?

....

30   Venison is the flesh of deer. Which type of deer is most generally used?

....

31   Give the method of skinning, cleaning and cutting rabbit for stewing.

....

....

32   When cleaning a hare, why is it usual to reserve the blood?

....

33   The blood of a hare is contained in a compartment covered by a membrane at the front of the forequarter.   True/False

34   How can escalopes of rabbit be prepared?

....

35   When preparing a saddle of hare or rabbit the thin membrane covering the flesh must be removed.   True/False

36   Give two reasons why a saddle of hare might be larded.

....

....

37   Wild boar are kept in pens or allowed to free range. Which would have the more traditional flavour?

....

38 For tender cuts and joints, a young wild boar is best. What procedure should be adopted in the preparation of the meat from older animals to make it palatable?

....

39 Give two examples for the use of liver from game.

....

40 Give an example for the use of the hearts and kidneys.

....

41 What would you supply if requested for game to make 5 litres (1 gallon) of game stock?

....

42 Describe the boning of a quail.

....

....

....

3F6.4 *Cook and finish complex game and offal dishes*

1 Give a recipe and method for a game farce.

....

....

....

....

2 What mise-en-place is required for roast game birds?

....

3 Give the procedure for roasting and serving a small game bird, e.g. a grouse or partridge.

....

....

4 Why should game birds be served on a croûte of fried bread and what should this bread be fried in?

....

5 Outline a method of pot-roasting pheasant served with a suitable garnish.

....

....

6 Suggest a method of cooking and serving for each of the following:
Grouse:

....

Partridge:

....

Pheasant:

....

Woodcock:

....

Snipe:

....

Wild duck:

....

Teal:

....

Hare:

....

Venison:

....

Rabbit:

....

Wild boar:

....

7 List three common faults found when game is cooked and served and suggest how they can be minimised.

   a Overcooked.

   b ....

   c ....

8 What are the main contamination risks when cooking and storing game dishes and how can they be minimised?

   ....

   ....

   ....

   ....

9 How can the maximum nutritional value be retained during the cooking and storing of game dishes?

   ....

10   What are the requirements for holding/storing cooked game dishes?

....

11   Indicate points of quality in the following dishes to be served and set out a recipe for the salmi.
  Roast grouse:

....

  Salmi of pheasant:

....

....

....

  Jugged hare:

....

  Braised partridge:

....

12   Give a recipe for a forcemeat suitable for stuffing quails.

....

....

....

13   Suggest recipes using quails with garnish and names as they would appear on a menu.
  Roasted:

....

....

En casserole:

....

....

Any method of your choice:

....

....

14 Suggest recipes for partridge:
A young tender bird:

....

....

....

An older red-legged bird:

....

....

....

15 Woodcock and snipe are usually roasted.　　True/False

16 Wild duck and teal when roasted are usually cooked pink unless otherwise requested. Suggest two other ways of cooking and serving these birds.

....

....

17 What is the approximate cooking time for a roast haunch of venison, and is it usually cooked through or left pink in the centre?

....

18 Describe the general style of sauce or gravy that is usually served, and give an example of a suitable sauce.

....

19 Suggest the names of six interesting dishes that can be prepared using rabbit and write them as they would appear on the menu.

....

....

....

....

....

....

20 Give a recipe and method using your own ideas for:
   Rabbit pie:

....

....

....

   Saddle of rabbit:

....

....

....

21 Briefly give the stages in making jugged hare. After thickening the sauce with the blood why must it not be re-boiled? Describe the traditional garnish.

....

....

....

....

22 Suggest two recipes using venison escalopes.

....

....

23 Suggest two recipes using saddle of venison.

....

....

24 You have been supplied with a skinned, cleaned and well-hung carcass of a young wild boar. Outline the dishes you would suggest preparing from it.

....

....

....

25 Suggest four suitable alcoholic liquors suitable for using in game sauces.

....

26 Using your own ideas, suggest one way of cooking and serving:
    Venison, hare, rabbit or wild boar's liver:

....

....

    Venison, hare or wild boar's kidneys:

....

....

Venison, hare or wild boar's heart:

....

....

27 Write as it would appear on the menu a different dish of game using each of the following methods of cooking:

Grilling:...

Shallow frying:..

Stir-frying:...

Sautéeing:..

Baking:...

Deep frying:...

Hot smoking:...

Poaching:...

En papillote:..

Steaming:...

Roasting:..

Pot roasting:..

3F6.5 *Prepare complex poultry and offal dishes*

1 Discuss any current trends that you have observed in the preparation of poultry and offal dishes.

....

....

2 List six quality points relating to fresh poultry.

a The breast of the bird should be plump.

b ....

c ....

d ....

e ....

f ....

3 How should frozen and chilled poultry be assessed for quality?

....

....

4 Discuss methods of efficient portion control of poultry and how waste can be minimised.

....

....

5 What are the main contamination threats when preparing and storing poultry and offal dishes and how can these risks be minimised?

....

....

....

....

6 Considering the nutritional value of poultry, the flesh is more easily

.... than that of butcher's meat. It contains .... and is

therefore useful for building and .... body tissues and

providing............................... and .... The fat content is

.... and contains a high percentage of unsaturated acids.

7 State the storage/holding requirements for prepared uncooked poultry and offal.

....

....

8 Outline the relevant legislation relating to:

Preparation and storage: ....

Health and safety: ....

Food hygiene:..

9   It is essential that the cleanliness of preparation areas and equipment is fully maintained throughout the service in accordance with the relevant legislation. If you were in charge of this section of work with other people working under you, how would you ensure that this is carried out?

....

....

10   How can the nutritional value of poultry be affected during the preparation process?

....

....

11   In your experience what weight variation of turkey is available?

....

12   Turkey is cleaned and trussed in the same way as chicken but in addition two other things have to be done. What are these?

....

....

13   When in your opinion would it make sense to:

Clean, truss and leave a turkey whole: ....

Remove the legs and bone/stuff them: ....

Bone the turkey and legs, stuff and roll them:...

14   Give the weight and number of turkeys you would order for:

a 20 portions ....

b 500 portions ....

15   Give recipes for two traditional turkey stuffings.

....

....

....

16 Name two ways in which turkey liver can be utilised and the method of preparation for each.

....

....

....

....

17 Why is it essential for the wishbones of turkeys to be removed before the bird is trussed?

....

18 Why is it essential to remove the sinews from turkey legs? Describe in detail how this is done.

....

....

19 Name two interesting stuffings for ballottines of turkey.

....

20 Briefly explain the procedure for cleaning/drawing/eviscerating a bird.

Pick:...

Singe: ....

Neck: ....

Head: ....

Crop: ....

Vent:...

Loosen: ....

Draw: ....

Wipe:...

Gizzard:...

Liver: ....

Neck and heart:..

21 Why must the vent end of a bird be clean at all times?

....

22 When drawing innards carelessly, what would be the effect of the gall-bladder bursting?

....

23 What preparation is required to the liver?

....

24 How is a gizzard peeled, split and cleaned?

....

25 What three cleaned items of birds are used for stock?

....

26 Is it necessary to truss birds for roasting. Why?

....

27 Why is it necessary to remove the wishbone before cutting up a chicken for sauté?

....

28 What is the essential requirement with regard to the size of all the cut pieces?

....

29 Why should poultry carcasses be carefully cleaned and kept?

....

30 Briefly describe the preparation of a chicken for grilling.

....

....

31 What is a suitable weight of chicken for preparing suprêmes?

....

32 When preparing suprêmes after the legs have been removed, what two items are next removed?

....

33 If the fillets and the .... are not removed from suprêmes, what would be likely to happen when the suprêmes are cooked?

....

34 When the trimmed chicken fillet is replaced in the suprême, what is the reason for using a bat?

....

35 Briefly outline the procedure for making chicken ballottines.

....

....

36 How would raw chicken be cut for the following dishes?

Fricassée:...

Stir-fry:...

37 Name two dishes for which raw chicken could be diced.

....

38 State a recipe for chicken forcemeat.

....

39 Explain the differences between the preparation for chicken mousse, mousselines, quenelles and soufflé.

....

....

....

40 How are chicken livers prepared for:
An egg dish, e.g. omelette or scrambled eggs:

....

Canapé Diane:

....

Pilaff with chicken livers:

....

41 Give two examples of marinades suitable for two different chicken dishes of your choice.

....

....

42 List the quality points for a tender duck or goose.

....

....

43 When cleaning out a duck or goose, there is one difference in the cleaning of the giblets compared to a chicken or turkey. What is this?

....

44 Why is it not necessary to remove the livers from pigeons when they are drawn and cleaned?

....

3F6.6 *Cook and finish complex poultry and offal dishes*

1 What current trends have you noticed in cooking poultry and offal dishes?

....

....

....

2 Suggest a different dish of poultry and write it as it would appear on the menu for each of the following methods of cookery.

Grilling:..

Shallow frying:...

Stir-frying:...

Sautéeing:...

Baking:..

Deep frying:..

Hot smoking:...

Poaching:..

Steaming:..

En papillote:..

Roasting:...

Pot roasting:...

3 What are the main contamination risks when cooking and storing poultry and offal dishes and how can they be minimised?

....

....

....

4 How can the maximum nutritional value be retained during the cooking of poultry and offal dishes?

....

5 Discuss the storage/holding requirements for cooked poultry and offal dishes.

....

....

6 What are the *detailed* quality points you would look for in the following?
Hot chicken soufflé:

....

Chicken sauté Archiduc:

....

Suprême of chicken with asparagus:

....

Braised duck with celery:

....

Roast duckling:

....

Breast of duckling with pineapple:

....

Casscrole of guinea fowl:

....

Hot roast turkey:

....

Hot roast goose:

....

7 Using your own ideas, how would you enhance any of these dishes by appropriate presentation?

....

....

....

....

8 State the relevant health and safety legislation points and food hygiene legislation in relation to the cooking of poultry and offal dishes.

....

....

9 List the bad practices that you have observed with regard to question 8.

....

....

....

....

10 Assuming that you are in charge of the section responsible for cooking poultry, how would you ensure that the cooking areas and equipment were kept clean and fully maintained during service? Write out your answer as a check list to be seen by all your assistants.

....

....

....

....

11 What is your attitude to the following statement: 'The customer is always right.' Discuss this in relation to a customer asking for a number of adjustments to one of your standard recipes.

....

....

....

12 If you are in charge of a busy section with two to three assistants, how can you ensure that all cooked and finished dishes fully meet with recipe specifications?

....

....

13 How would you ensure that cooked poultry and offal dishes not for immediate consumption are stored in accordance with recipe specification and relevant legislation?

....

....

14 Name the different ways of cooking stuffing to be served with roast turkey. Which method would you use for a whole 5 kg (10 lb) bird to be served and carved at table, for 250 plated portions and for 500 portions in services of 10?

....

....

....

15 What is the alternative to cooking and peeling chestnuts for chestnut stuffing?

....

16 What is the approximate cooking time per lb for roast turkey?

....

17 Why is frequent basting recommended when roasting turkeys?

....

18 What would be the effect on roast turkey if it were covered in fat bacon and sealed in foil?

....

19 What is the method of checking that a turkey is cooked?

....

20 For roast turkey to be served in traditional style, up to seven accompaniments and garnishes may be served. Name them.

....

....

....

21 Why should a roast turkey be allowed to stand for 10–15 minutes before being carved?

....

22 Describe how you would carve a whole hot 20 kg (20 lb) turkey.

....

....

23 What is the danger of carving turkey too far in advance and how can this be avoided?

....

24 What are the two signs to check whether a roast chicken is cooked?

....

25 Using your own ideas, give a recipe for an interesting stuffing for roast chicken.

....

....

26 There are numerous standard recipes for dishes of chicken sauté. Give two recipes using your own ideas.

....

....

....

....

27 Describe the cooking and serving of devilled grilled chicken.

....

....

....

28 Why is it essential when cooking a chicken pie to ensure that the stock is well flavoured?

....

29 Give three recipes for a dish of chicken suprêmes, one to be cooked white, one brown and one breadcrumbed.

....

....

....

....

....

....

30 Taking a 2½kg (5 lb) boiling chicken, state the various uses to which it can be put.

....

....

....

....

31 Chicken à la king is a standard recipe. Give two variations on it using your own ideas.

....

....

....

....

32 What are the important points to ensure the cooking and serving of a quality chicken vol-au-vent?

....

....

33 Give two recipes using your own ideas for chicken in casserole.

....

....

....

....

34 Give two recipes of your choosing for stuffed, crumbed chicken suprêmes.

....

....

....

....

35 Give two recipes for chicken ballottines.

....

....

....

....

36 Briefly describe four ways of cooking and serving hot dishes of chicken livers.

....

....

....

....

37 Briefly describe the cooking and serving of roast duck and roast goose.

....

....

....

....

38 Suggest and briefly describe two dishes of braised duck.

....

....

....

....

39 Outline the method of cooking and serving duck à l'orange.

....

....

40 What is the nature of the flesh of guinea fowl and what steps need to be considered when cooking it?

....

....

41 Suggest a recipe for each of the following:
    Guinea fowl in casserole:

....

....

Sauté of guinea fowl:

....

....

Suprême of guinea fowl:

....

....

42 Describe the cooking and serving of chicken mousselines and two suitable sauces.

....

....

....

....

43 Suggest two additional ingredients that could be added to a hot chicken mousse.

....

Record of Achievement – Completion of Unit 3F6

Candidate's signature ....

Assessor's signature ....

Date ....

Unit 3F7

Prepare, cook and finish hot sauces, soups and cold dressings

3F7.1 *Prepare, cook and finish hot sauces, stocks and gravies*

1   What current trends in the preparation of hot sauces have you observed over the past few years?

   ....

   ....

2   Unless quality ingredients are used to make stocks, gravies and sauces, then a quality product will not be produced. Discuss this and list examples.

   ....

   ....

   ....

3   What are the main contamination threats when making and storing stocks, sauces and gravies and how can these be minimised?

   ....

   ....

   ....

   ....

4   After making a stock or sauce that is required for the following day, what is the correct procedure?

   ....

5 How can quality be assessed in the following finished products?
White stock:

....

Brown stock:

....

Roast gravy:

....

Thickened gravy:

....

Hollandaise sauce:

....

Béarnaise sauce:

....

Broccoli sauce:

....

Suprême sauce:

....

Fish sauce made from a reduction:

....

Yoghurt thickened sauce:

....

Shellfish coulis sauce:

....

Oil-based sauce:

....

6   What are the storage/holding requirements for cooked stocks, gravies and sauces?

....

....

7   Outline the relevant health and safety legislation and the relevant food hygiene
     legislation for the cooking and storage of stocks, gravies and sauces.

....

....

....

....

8   Assuming that you are in charge of the section responsible for the cooking of stocks,
     gravies and sauces, how would you ensure that the cleanliness of preparation and
     cooking areas and equipment is fully maintained throughout the production period
     in accordance with relevant legislation? Set out your answer as a staff instruction.

....

....

....

....

9   To produce top-quality, well-flavoured meat stock, what is/are the basic essential
     ingredient(s)?

....

....

10   What is meant by a stock with 'body'?

....

11 What are the essential points to produce a completely clean clear stock?

....

....

12 Give a recipe and the method for a rich, well-flavoured brown stock.

....

....

....

13 What are the approximate cooking times for:

Beef stock: ....

Chicken stock: ....

Fish stock: ....

14 What basic ingredients are required to produce a quality chicken stock?

....

....

15 Give a recipe for a well-flavoured vegetable stock.

....

....

....

16 Name the best bones for a well-flavoured fish stock.

....

17 What is the effect of overcooking a fish stock?

....

18 Set out a recipe for a quality shellfish stock.

....

....

....

19 How is colour achieved when making a shellfish stock?

....

20 Describe the making, storing and uses for glazes?

....

....

21 Briefly set out the method of making roast gravy from a roast joint or bird. Indicate the vital points for producing a quality gravy.

....

....

....

22 Outline the procedure for producing roast gravy for 750 portions of roast beef.

....

....

....

23 What is the best ingredient for thickening a jus lié and why?

....

24 What are the quality points in a jus lié?

....

....

25 Set out the basic points in making a hollandaise sauce.

....

....

....

26 What is the proportion of egg yolks to butter for hollandaise sauce?

....

27 What is the proportion of egg yolks to butter for béarnaise sauce?

....

28 Why is there a difference between questions 26 and 27?

....

29 List the causes and remedies for a curdled egg-based sauce.

....

....

....

30 What steps can be taken to stabilise a large quantity of an egg-based sauce?

....

....

31 Discuss the risks of salmonella infection and how they can be reduced when making and keeping warm egg-based sauces.

....

....

32 The classical repertoire lists a number of variations for egg-based sauces. Using your own ideas, suggest two variations for hollandaise sauce and two for béarnaise sauce, and state the dishes you would serve them with.

....

....

....

....

33 Describe the method of making two each of the following sauces and suggest dishes
with which they could be served in each case.
Fruit:

....

....

....

Pulse:

....

....

....

Vegetable:

....

....

....

34 Name three types of food suitable for a cream-based sauce.

....

35 State how cream can be used in the finishing of a fish sauce from a reduction.

....

....

36   What base sauces can be used to form a cream sauce?

....

....

37   The contemporary style of sauces for many fish, meat, poultry and game dishes is to reduce the cooking liquor until it has the lightest possible consistency. List the advantages of this type of sauce and name the dangers.

....

....

....

38   When and why are yoghurt or fromage frais used to thicken sauces? Give two examples and name the dishes they could accompany.

....

....

....

39   A shellfish coulis sauce is usually made from .... or ....

40   When making a shellfish coulis sauce, why is it essential to pound thoroughly the soft shells and why should they initially be well sweated in the butter or oil?

....

41   Briefly set out the method of making a shellfish coulis sauce:
        Using live crayfish:

....

....

....

Using cooked lobster shell:

....

....

....

42 How is a sauce thickened by blood? Explain this in detail. What can happen if the correct procedure is not followed? Give one example of a dish in which the sauce is thickened in this way.

....

....

....

....

43 Any sauce made from a roux base can use a good quality oil in place of butter or margarine for the roux. Name six oil-based sauces.

....

....

....

44 Give an example of use for each of the following:
Monter au beurre:

....

Liaison:

....

Glazing:

....

Addition of herbs:

....

Addition of blood:

....

Addition of cooking liquors:

....

Emulsifying:

....

Clarifying:

....

Liquidising/blending:

....

Binding:

....

Reduction:

....

3F7.2 *Prepare and finish cold savoury sauces, dressings and jellies*

1 What current trends have you observed in connection with cold savoury sauces, dressings and aspic jellies?

....

....

....

2 When selecting an oil and vinegar for cold sauces, what would be your criteria and why?

....

....

3 What are the main contamination threats when making and storing cold sauces and dressings and how can they be minimised? Draw up a check list for staff to follow.

....

....

....

....

4 What are the storage/holding requirements for prepared sauces?

....

....

5 Where should a freshly made mayonnaise be stored and how does this affect the quantity to be made?

....

6 How is quality identified in the following?
Mayonnaise:

....

Vinaigrette:

....

Tartare sauce:

....

Horseradish sauce:

....

Mint sauce:

....

Cumberland sauce:

....

Aspic jelly:

....

7 What are current government guidelines on nutrition related to cold sauces, dressings and jellies?

....

....

....

8 It is accepted that aspic jelly is an ideal medium for the growth of micro-organisms. Discuss the implications of this.

....

....

9 How would you ensure that the cleanliness of preparation and cooking areas and equipment is fully maintained throughout the service in accordance with relevant legislation? Set out your answer in the form of instruction to all staff to be printed and displayed in an appropriate place.

....

....

....

....

10 To produce a good-quality, well-flavoured aspic jelly, it is essential to start with a good quality, well flavoured ....

11 List the points of procedure in making aspic jelly.

....

....

....

12 When using leaf gelatine, why is it necessary to soak it in cold water, and for how long should it be soaked?

....

13 If, in spite of the care taken in its preparation, the aspic jelly is not crystal clear, how can this be remedied?

....

14 Aspic jelly should be strained through a fine chinois.   True/False

15 Bearing in mind that aspic jelly is one of the most dangerous potential mediums for the growth of micro-organisms, how should this be reflected in the quality of the ingredients used in the making of aspic jelly?

....

....

16 What are micro-organisms?

....

17 Aspic jelly should be produced with a flavour that will complement the food it is to be used with. Name three flavours.

....

18 Outline the procedure for producing aspic jelly flavoured with wine.

....

....

....

19 Gelatine is an animal-based product and not suitable for vegetarian dishes. What is the name of the alternative product and from what is it produced?

....

20 State four uses for aspic jelly naming specific dishes in each case.

....

....

....

....

21 Briefly summarise seven points to be observed whe using aspic jelly.

....

....

....

....

....

....

....

22 Name five types of oil and three types of vinegar suitable for use in cold dressings.

....

....

....

....

....

23 List three seasonings that may be used in vinaigrette.

....

24 If required to produce fresh, herb-flavoured vinaigrette, which herbs would you choose?

....

25 If vinegar is not wanted in a vinaigrette, what could be used as a substitute?

....

26 Is it possible to keep the oil and vinegar in a vinaigrette completely blended? What follows from your answer with regard to each time the vinaigrette is to be used?

....

27 Roquefort dressing is a variation of vinaigrette. Name two other cheeses that could be used in place of Roquefort.

....

28 Name the additions to a vinaigrette to make thousand island dressing.

....

....

29 Using your own ideas, suggest three variations to a basic vinaigrette.

....

....

....

30 The sharpness of a vinaigrette is determined by the amount of vinegar used and by individual preference. What do you consider a sensible proportion of oil to vinegar?

....

31 In some instances it may be preferable to dress a dish using the lightest quantity of a top quality oil and, depending on the dish, this may be done in the kitchen or by the customer at table. Give four examples.

....

....

....

....

32 Give the recipe that you use to make mayonnaise.

....

....

....

33 Give four reasons why a mayonnaise may curdle and how this can be rectified.

....

....

....

....

34 Using your own ideas, give three variations to a mayonnaise.

....

....

....

35 What is an alternative to vinegar in the making of mayonnaise?

....

36 How is sour cream dressing made? Give four examples of its use.

....

....

....

....

37 When and why would a yoghurt or fromage frais dressing be used? What could it replace?

....

....

38 Give four examples of its use.

....

....

....

....

39 Describe the preparation of two fruit and two vegetable-based sauces and suggest dishes with which they could be served.

....

....

....

....

40 Is there any reason why fruit or vegetable-based sauces could not be used as dressings for certain foods or mixtures of foods? Support your answer with examples.

....

....

3F7.3 *Prepare, cook and finish soups*

1 What current trends have you observed with regard to the preparation and cooking of soups?

....

....

....

2 If top quality soups are to be produced, why is it essential to use quality ingredients? Discuss this point in the light of your own experience.

....

....

3 State methods of portion control and minimising waste of soups, giving suggestions of portion size for:

Lunch: ....

Dinner: ....

Supper: ....

4 How should the maximum nutritional value be retained during the preparation and cooking of soups? Give examples of how it can be lost.

....

....

5 What are the main contamination threats when making and storing soups and how can they be minimised? Give examples of any bad practices that you have observed.

....

....

....

....

6 List the quality points for assessing:
Cream soups:

....

Velouté:

....

Purée:

....

Consommé:

....

Cold soup:

....

Fruit soup:

....

Broth:

....

Chowder:

....

Brown soup:

....

Bortsch:

....

Bouillabaisse:

....

Bisque:

....

Minestrone:

....

7 State the storage/holding requirements for soups.

....

....

8 What are the current government guidelines on nutrition?

....

....

9 For economic reasons, the seasons, availability and prices of certain foods should be considered when planning to make soups. Suggest three examples and give reasons.

....

....

....

10 Outline the relevant health and safety and food hygiene legislation relating to the preparation and cooking of soups.

....

....

....

11 How should soups not for immediate consumption be stored in accordance with recipe specifications and relevant legislation?

....

....

12 How should the cleanliness of preparation and cooking areas and equipment be fully maintained throughout the service in accordance with relevant legislation? Draw up a list of points for all staff to be displayed in the working area.

....

....

....

....

13 Suggest three different methods of making cream soups.

....

....

....

14 Using your own ideas, give a brief recipe for each and name them as they would appear on a menu.

....

....

....

....

....

....

15 Suggest three different ways of finishing cream soup.

....

....

16 Describe the correct texture and consistency of a cream soup.

....

....

17 Describe the difference between a velouté and a cream soup.

....

....

18 Give three examples of velouté soups including a brief method for cach.

....

....

....

....

....

....

19 State the traditional addition and finish of a velouté soup.

....

20 The texture and consistency of a velouté should be the same as for a cream soup.   True/False

21 Give a brief description of a purée soup.

....

....

22 Give examples of three popular purée soups and any accompaniments of your choice.

....

....

23 Should the consistency of a purée soup be different from that of a cream soup or velouté?

....

24 Set out the ingredients required to produce 4 litres (1 gallon) each of the following consommés:

Fish	Meat	Poultry	Game	Vegetable

25 What is the procedure for producing a crystal clear consommé?

....

....

....

26 If a consommé is not clear, what is the remedy?

....

27 The flavour of a finished consommé will depend mainly on the quality of the stock used.   True/False

28 Describe the correct finish and appearance of a beef consommé.

....

....

29 There should be no signs of fat on the surface of a consommé. How can this be achieved?

....

....

30 Describe the process of clarification and list six possible errors.

....

....

....

....

31 Suggest two interesting garnishes for each of the following consommés.

Fish: ....

Meat: ....

Poultry: ....

Game: ....

Vegetable: ....

32 If a consommé is to be flavoured with a liquor, e.g. sherry or Madeira, when should this be added?

....

33 Suggest a suitable liquor for each of the following consommés.

Fish: ....

Meat: ....

Poultry: ....

Game: ....

34 Suggest a suitable consommé, naming it as it would appear on a menu for:
Lunch for 250 given for a royal visitor in the city of London in October:

....

A dinner party for six in June:

....

A midnight supper in January:

....

35 What is a 'royal'?

....

36 Why is a royal often used for consommé garnish?

....

37 Briefly describe the preparation, cooking and use of a royal.

....

....

38 Why should a vegetable julienne garnish be cut no longer than 2 cm (1 in)?

....

39 A cold consommé should be lightly jellied when served. Should this slight jellying be caused by the addition of gelatine or the quality of the stock? Explain your answer.

....

....

40 Suggest two interesting cold consommés.

....

41 Other than vichyssoise, suggest two other interesting cold soups.

....

42 What action would you take if a customer requested a portion of vichyssoise served hot?

....

43 Give four examples of fruit soups, two hot, two cold.

....

....

44 What is an essential requirement of the fruit to be used for an uncooked soup?

....

45 Using your own ideas, name and give the recipes for:
A cold fruit soup to be served for a special lunch for six in July:

....

....

....

A hot fruit soup to be served for lunch in December:

....

....

....

46 Name any fruits that you would consider unsuitable for fruit soups and state why in each case.

....

....

....

47 Describe a quality broth.

....

....

48   List the quantities of ingredients required to produce 4 litres (1 gallon) of each of the following.

Chicken broth	Mutton broth	Scotch broth

49   You have been requested to produce a game broth. State your recipe and include a garnish.

....

....

....

50   Give a sample definition for a chowder.

....

51   From where do chowders originate?

....

52   Name four types of fish typically used for chowders.

....

....

53   Which fish is the most popular for use in chowders?

....

54 Having read and studied a recipe for clam chowder, use your own ideas to write a recipe. Keep to the general characteristics of a chowder and use locally obtained fish.

....

....

....

55 Name three interesting brown soups.

....

....

56 Give a recipe for a brown soup of your own choice with a garnish and to be finished with a liquor.

....

....

....

57 Should the consistency of a brown soup be different from that of a cream soup and, if so, why?

....

58 Give a brief description of bortsch.

....

....

59 What is the dominant vegetable flavour in a bortsch?

....

60 What are the traditional accompaniments?

....

....

61 In France, the liquid of a bouillabaisse is sometimes served as soup followed by the fish as the next course. Having studied a recipe for this dish and considered numerous variations, set out a 4 litre (1 gallon) soup recipe using your own ideas, keeping the general character of the dish and using locally obtained fish.

....

....

....

....

62 Give the definition of a bisque.

....

63 Suggest which fish are suitable for a bisque. Which is the most popular?

....

....

64 If a good quantity of soft lobster shell is available, is it necessary to use whole lobster for making bisque? Explain your answer giving your reasons why.

....

....

65 Describe how you would assess a lobster bisque for quality.

....

....

66 Lobster bisque is sometimes finished with cream and brandy. In your opinion should this be added in the kitchen or should the customer be asked in the restaurant if they would like either or both of these additions?

....

67 List the foreign soups with which you are familiar and give the country of origin in each case.

....

....

....

....

68 Soups can be varied by using combinations of ingredients, e.g. tomato and potato. Suggest four interesting combinations of soups together with garnishes of your choice (if necessary).

....

....

....

....

69 Name your four favourite herbs and suggest a soup with which each could be used.

....

....

70 Name four spices and suggest suitable soups with which they could be used.

....

....

Record of Achievement – Completion of Unit 3F7

Candidate's signature   ....

Assessor's signature   ....

Date   ....

Unit 3F8

Prepare, cook and finish complex vegetable dishes

3F8.1 *Prepare complex vegetable dishes*

1   What current trends have you observed with regard to the preparation of vegetable dishes?

....

....

....

2   Give a simple definition of a vegetarian and a vegan and describe how their diets are affected.

....

....

3   List the quality points relating to raw and frozen vegetables.

....

....

....

4   Name the factors that contribute to the spoilage of fresh vegetables.

....

....

5   Assuming you are in charge of a large section responsible for vegetable production with a number of assistants, how would you ensure that minimum waste and portion

control are made?

....

....

6 What is the nutritional value of root and green vegetables?

....

....

7 Good cooking can retain maximum nutritional value. Careless cooking can destroy nutrients in vegetables. List the good and bad points.

....

....

....

8 How should uncooked vegetable dishes be stored/held?

....

....

9 What are the current government guidelines on nutrition?

....

....

10 How can you keep up to date with the seasonal variations in quality, availability and price of vegetables?

....

....

11 List the relevant health and safety and food hygiene legislation relating to the preparation of vegetables and complex vegetable dishes.

....

....

....

12 How should the cleanliness of preparation areas and equipment be fully maintained throughout the service in accordance with current legislation?

....

....

13 Why is it important to select the type, quality and quantity of specific vegetables for recipe specifications? Support your answer with examples.

....

....

....

14 Where possible, an existing recipe should be adjusted to meet a customer's expressed requirement. Discuss this statement and give examples.

....

....

15 List examples for each of the following types of vegetables and give the method of preparation in each case.
     Roots (six examples):

....

....

....

....

....

....

     Tubers (four examples):

....

....

....

....

Bulbs (four examples):

....

....

....

....

Leaves (six examples):

....

....

....

....

....

....

Stems (six examples):

....

....

....

....

....

....

Flower heads (two examples):

....

....

Fungi (six examples):

....

....

....

....

....

....

Fruits (vegetable, six examples):

....

....

....

....

....

....

Pods and seeds (six examples):

....

....

....

....

....

....

Pulses (six examples):

....

....

....

....

....

....

16 Suggest two vegetables which can be made into hot mousses and two suitable for cold mousses.

....

....

17 Give the method of preparation of one hot and one cold mousse and suggest two ways in which each could be served, writing the names as they would appear on the menu.

....

....

18 Give the method of preparing a vegetable royal.

....

....

19 Suggest three vegetables suitable for preparation as royals.

....

20 Suggest a use for each of the three royals.

....

....

....

21 There are various ways of moulding vegetables, e.g. subrics of spinach. Suggest three ways of moulding vegetables and indicate a use for each.

....

....

....

22 What are the two essential requirements for preparing globe artichokes into fonds?

....

....

23 Outline the preparation of a globe artichoke to be served whole.

....

....

24 What is a 'blanc' and what is its function?

....

25 What are the important points of preparation of asparagus?

....

....

26 How are aubergines, courgettes and peppers prepared for ratatouille?

....

....

....

27 What preparation is required for young kohlrabi to be served whole?

....

....

28 How many types of broccoli are there and how does the preparation of each differ?

....

....

....

29 Which of the following should be peeled with a knife or a peeler?

Potatoes: .... Carrots: ....

Turnips: .... Parsnips: ....

Swedes: .... Mooli: ....

Celeriac: .... Salsify: ....

30 Briefly describe the preparation of celery for braising.

....

....

31 Describe the preparation of:
Cabbage for serving as plain cabbage:

....

....

Cabbage for braised cabbage:

....

....

Spring greens:

....

....

32 For quality service, what type of Brussels sprouts would you order and why?

....

33 What preparation is required for seakale?

....

....

34 Name six vegetables suitable for stuffing and give the ingredients suitable for the stuffing in each case.

....

....

....

....

....

....

35 What are the four quality points for the selection of bean sprouts?

....

....

36 Describe cardoons and indicate how they are prepared.

....

....

37 Describe the christophine, give its three other names and describe its preparation.

....

....

....

38 Give the characteristics of the mooli, its high water content, how it can be reduced and how it is prepared.

....

....

....

39 What are the two other names for okra?

....

40 Describe the flavour of okra.

....

41 How is okra prepared?

....

....

42 By what other names is scorzonera known?

....

43 Describe the flavour of scorzonera.

....

44 How are fresh salsify selected?

....

How is salsify prepared?

....

....

45 What are the points of quality when selecting squash?

....

....

46 What is the difference in the skins of summer squash and winter squash and why?

....

....

47 Give the alternative name for Swiss chard.

....

48 Describe the flavour and appearance of Swiss chard.

....

49 Explain the similarities between yams, potatoes and sweet potatoes.

....

....

50 Why nutritionally should potatoes be peeled as thinly as possible and as close to the service time as possible?

....

51 There are a number of vegetarian recipes for which little or no cooking is required, such as tofu pâté with raw vegetables. Using your own ideas, suggest two recipes suitable for vegetarians in which no cooking is required.

....

....

52 Certain vegetables may be marinated, such as aubergine, peppers for grilling, and pulse beans for salads. Ingredients for marinades may include oil, vinegar, herbs, spice, garlic, lemon juice and ginger. Suggest two vegetable dishes of your own choice and a suitable marinade for each.

....

....

53 What are the essential requirements for turning or carving vegetables?

....

....

54 Suggest three vegetables suitable for carving and indicate the procedure you would adopt for each.

....

....

....

3F8.2 *Cook, regenerate and finish complex vegetable dishes*

1 What current trends have you observed in the cooking and regenerating of complex vegetable dishes?

....

....

2 State the effects of cooking on the nutritional content and chemical structure of vegetables.

....

....

3 What are the storage/holding requirements for cooked vegetable dishes?

....

....

4 Indicate how you would assess for quality in the following:
Artichoke bottoms with spinach and cheese sauce:

....

Stir fried bean sprouts:

....

Stuffed kohlrabi:

....

Buttered leeks:

....

Stewed okra:

....

Salsify fritters:

....

Subrics of spinach:

....

Leaf spinach with pine nuts and garlic:

....

Stuffed aubergines:

....

Stuffed tomatoes:

....

Morels in oil, herbs and garlic:

....

Yam soufflé:

....

Bubble and squeak:

....

Pommes Elisabeth:

....

Pommes champignol:

....

Pommes savoyarde:

....

Pommes dauphinoise:

....

Rösti potatoes:

....

5 State the relevant health and safety and food hygiene legislation in relation to cooked and regenerated vegetable dishes.

....

....

....

6   Assuming that you are in charge of a busy vegetable section with assistants, produce a schedule stating how the cooking areas and equipment are to be kept clean and fully maintained throughout the service in accordance with relevant legislation.

....

....

....

....

7   The nutritional value of vegetables is affected by bad cooking and lost by overcooking. How can nutrients be adequately retained during cooking? Give examples of bad practice that you have observed.

....

....

....

8   How can the maximum quality of a vegetable dish be retained during cooking, regenerating and finishing?

....

....

9   To comply with relevant legislation, how should products not required for immediate consumption be stored?

....

....

10   How is a top-quality roast potato produced?

....

....

11 How important is the selection of the type of potato? Give examples.

....

....

12 How would you create slight variation in roast potatoes other than by shape?

....

....

13 What other vegetables are suitable for roasting?

....

....

14 Baked jacket potatoes are one of the most nutritious forms of potato. Using your own ideas, suggest three ways of using baked jacket potatoes for a quality establishment.

....

....

....

15 What other vegetables are suitable for baking?

....

....

16 List the basic principles for quality shallow-frying of vegetables.

....

....

....

17 Outline the cooking and service of lyonnaise potatoes.

....

....

....

18 Suggest from your own ideas three methods of cooking shallow-fried potatoes from new potatoes and from cooked potatoes.

....

....

....

19 Which is the best way of cooking potatoes for sauté and why?
    Peeled and boiled:

....

    Boiled in skins:

....

    Peeled and steamed:

....

    Steamed in skins:

....

    Peeled, sliced and part boiled:

....

    Peeled, sliced and half-steamed:

....

20 Name three other vegetables that can be shallow fried from raw and three that are best part boiled before shallow frying.

....

....

....

21 What are the differences (if any) between cooking a dish of shallow-fried and stir-fried vegetables?

....

....

22 Describe two interesting ways of cooking a dish of stir-fried vegetables, listing the ingredients in each case.

....

....

....

....

23 What is the difference between shallow frying and sautéeing?

....

24 Name three examples for each of the following:
   Deep-fried potato dish:

....

   Deep-fried vegetable dish:

....

   Deep-fried vegetable fritter:

....

25 Set out a check list for your section of the correct techniques for deep frying and list the possible dangers and how they can be avoided. Name the correct five precautions and appliances which must be at hand.

....

....

....

....

....

....

....

....

....

....

26 List the correct procedure for boiling potatoes and vegetables.

....

....

27 Name the faults that you have observed when boiling potatoes and vegetables and the effect on the vegetables.

....

....

....

28 Numerous vegetables are suitable for braising, e.g. celery, onions and leeks. Give a list of other vegetables that could be braised together with the methods.

....

....

....

....

29 Vegetables can be stewed, usually in combinations, e.g. ratatouille. What other combinations could you use and what herb or spice additions might be made?

....

....

....

30 Give the method and advantages of steaming certain vegetables, indicating those vegetables that you would prefer to steam rather than boil and giving your reasons why.

....

....

....

....

31 A definition of poaching is the cooking of foods in the minimum of liquid, which is not allowed to boil but kept as near to boiling point as possible. Considering potatoes and any other vegetables, suggest four dishes that could be cooked by poaching and give brief recipes in each case.

....

....

....

....

....

....

32 What are the two ways of grilling vegetables?

....

33 For what type of occasion are grilled vegetables ideally suitable?

....

34 Name a selection of vegetables that can be grilled from raw.

....

35 Name a selection of vegetables that need to be parboiled before grilling.

....

36 Give the method of grilling vegetables and suggest ways of varying the flavour.

....

....

37 Give five ways in which vegetables can be prepared and cooked for use as garnish to other dishes.
    a Deep-fried fine julienne of root vegetables.

    b Thinly sliced root vegetables deep fried as crisps.

    c ....

    d ....

    e ....

38 Using your own ideas, give two recipes for each of the following and suggest suitable accompaniments.
    Vegetable mousse:

....

....

Vegetable royale:

....

....

Vegetable mould:

....

....

39 Give examples of the vegetables suitable for regeneration by the following methods. Briefly describe the method and the reasons why regeneration may be used in each case.

Steaming:

....

....

Microwave:

....

....

Combi-steaming:

....

....

Grilling:

....

....

Sautéeing:

....

....

Baking:

....

....

Boiling:

....

....

Shallow frying:

....

....

Deep frying:

....

....

40 Suggest four vegetables suitable for being stuffed, the stuffing in each case and how they can be cooked.

....

....

....

....

....

....

....

....

41 Assume you are working in a country house hotel and the policy at dinner is to serve a side dish of vegetables on a plate to each customer to accompany the main course. Suggest the selections (1 potato, 3 vegetables) you would offer over a 7-day period.

Day 1:

....

....

Day 2:

....

....

Day 3:

....

....

Day 4:

....

....

Day 5:

....

....

Day 6:

....

....

Day 7:

....

....

42 As vegetarianism increases in popularity, so the need for starter and main course vegetable dishes becomes more important. Name three dishes and give the ingredients and recipe in each case.

First or starter courses, vegetarian:

....

....

....

....

....

....

First or starter courses, vegan:

....

....

....

....

....

....

Main courses, vegetarian:

....

....

....

....

....

....

Main courses, vegan:

....

....

....

....

....

....

43 Give two examples of vegetable dishes that can be served in pastry.

....

Record of Achievement – Completion of Unit 3F8

Candidate's signature ....

Assessor's signature ....

Date ....

Unit 3F9

Prepare, cook and present cold buffet items

3F9.1 *Prepare cold buffet items*

1 What current trends have you observed in the preparation of cold buffet items?

....

....

2 What are the important quality points relating to the main ingredients of cold buffets?

....

....

3 What are the main contamination threats when preparing and storing buffet items and how can these be minimised?

....

....

....

....

4 Name the storage/heating requirements for prepared buffet items?

....

....

5 How would you assess for quality in prepared buffet items?

....

....

6 Assuming that you are in charge of the cold buffet section with assistants, write a schedule for the cleanliness and maintenance of preparation areas and equipment throughout the service in accordance with relevant legislation.

....

....

....

....

7 How would you ensure that the selection, type and quality of ingredients are always in accord with recipe specifications? Indicate the importance of this in relation to the quality of your work.

....

....

8 How can the nutritional value of all ingredients be adequately retained during preparation? Give examples of how nutrients can be lessened or lost.

....

....

....

9 How flexible should you be with regard to your recipes when customers request considerable variation?

....

10 How should products not for immediate consumption be stored in accordance with recipe specifications and relevant legislation? Support your answer with six examples.

....

....

....

....

....

....

11 What are the important points to be borne in mind when preparing joints of meat to be carved on a buffet?

....

....

12 What preparation, if any, is required for a ham prior to cooking? Explain your answer.

....

....

13 What preparation is required for the following prior to cooking?
    Ox tongue:

....

....

    Wing rib of beef:

....

....

    Saddle of lamb:

....

....

    Suckling pig:

....

....

    Stuffed loin of veal:

....

....

14 You are required to prepare 150 portions of cold salmon to be presented whole. What order would you give to the fishmonger for the fish?

....

15 Describe the preparation of the salmon for cooking.

....

....

16 A 3 kg (6 lb) crawfish is requested to be cooked, dressed and served whole. What preparation is required for cooking?

....

....

17 100 portions of cold half-lobster are required as a first course on a buffet. What would your fish order be?

....

18 A 15 kg (30 lb) turkey has been delivered undrawn.
   a State the preparation required to prepare it for roasting for cold buffet.

....

....

   b Give an alternative method of preparation and explain the circumstances in which one or the other could be used.

....

....

19 Twelve cold roast chickens and six whole chickens to be boiled for dressing in chaudfroid are required. As both the roast chicken and the chicken chaudfroid are to be presented whole, describe the differences in preparation and trussing and explain why these are necessary.

....

....

....

....

20 Briefly describe the preparation of a 2 kg (4 lb) dressed crab.

....

....

21 You are required to produce a dish of cold savoury appetisers for a party of twelve, giving six varieties. Draw a shape for each appetiser, giving its size and naming the topping.

22 The order is for cold appetisers for 1,000 people.
  a Give your suggested items and number of varieties.

....

....

....

  b The party is for 8 pm Saturday evening. When would you start preparation? Detail your answer.

....

....

23 Briefly set out the preparation for cooking required for chicken galantine.

....

....

24 Suggest two dishes of stuffed fish suitable for a buffet.

....

25 Give the name and size of each stuffed fish dish.

....

....

26 Give the method of preparation for the cooking of each stuffed fish dish.

....

....

....

....

27 List the ingredients for the stuffing of each stuffed fish dish.

....

....

....

....

28 Using your own ideas, give the methods of preparation for fish encased in pastry indicating the size, preparation and type of pastry.
  One whole fish:

....

....

Individual portions:

....

....

29 You are required to be able to offer six compound salads on the menu.
   a Name your selection.

....

....

   b Indicate the mise-en-place you would organise.

....

....

30 Using your own ideas, list three interesting cold mousses and give a brief recipe for each.

....

....

....

....

....

31 List a selection of foods that you could offer smoked on a cold buffet.

....

....

....

32 What preparation is required prior to smoking for fish and meat items?

....

....

33 Describe the preparation of a side of smoked salmon to be ready for carving in the room.

....

....

34 Describe what you understand by the term canapé.

....

35 Indicate the various functions for which canapés may be requested.

....

....

36 Name six suggested bases.

....

....

....

....

....

....

37 Name four suggested toppings for each base you suggested.

....

....

....

....

38 Give your views on the use of aspic for glazing canapés or otherwise.

....

....

39 Describe the difference between a pâté and a terrine.

....

....

40 Give a method of preparation for each of your own choice.

....

....

41 Name two dishes for each of the following products to be served cold. Indicate the preparation required in each case.
   Vegetables:

....

....

   Fruits:

....

....

   Dairy products:

....

....

   Salad:

....

....

Fungi:

....

....

Eggs:

....

....

Rice:

....

....

Pasta:

....

....

42 Give two examples of use for each of the following preparation methods.
Pressing/reforming:

....

....

Shaping/moulding:

....

....

Rolling and stuffing:

....

....

Filleting:

....

....

Carving:

....

....

Deboning:

....

....

Trussing:

....

....

Tying:

....

....

Skinning:

....

....

Marinating:

....

....

Mincing:

....

....

Processing:

....

....

Blending:

....

....

43 State your views with examples on the following finishing methods.
Garnishing:

....

....

Decorating:

....

....

Piping:

....

....

Glazing:

....

....

Use of aspic jelly:

....

....

Dressing:

....

....

Carving:

....

....

44 You have been asked to prepare an interesting cold buffet for serving to an international gathering of 500 professional men and women at 1 pm on a Wednesday in June. Name your suggested menu with a brief description of dishes where necessary, together with a time schedule for the preparation. Include at least six items starred (*), suitable for vegetarians, and six starred (**), suitable for vegans. Continue on a separate sheet of paper if necessary.

....

....

....

....

....

....

....

....

3F9.2 *Cook cold buffet items*

1 Discuss any current trends that you have observed in the cooking of cold buffet items.

....

....

2 What are the main contamination threats when cooking and storing buffet items and how can they be minimised?

....

....

....

....

3 Name the storage/holding requirements and the most favourable conditions for cooked buffet products?

....

....

4 How can quality be assessed in the following cooked products?
    Terrine of game:

....

....

    Chicken pie:

....

....

5 State the relevant health and safety and food hygiene legislation relating to cooking of cold buffet items.

....

....

....

6 Set out a check list stating how the cleanliness of cooking areas and equipment is to be fully maintained throughout the service in accordance with relevant legislation.

....

....

....

....

7 How can you ensure that the nutritional value of products is adequately retained during cooking?

....

....

8 How do the correct methods of cooking maximise the quality of products? List examples of bad practice that you have observed.

....

....

....

....

9 To comply with relevant legislation, how should products not required for immediate consumption be stored so that the recipe specification and quality is not spoiled?

....

....

10 You have been requested to organise the smoking of your own foods.
   a Draw up a list of suggested items for hot smoking and for cold smoking.

....

....

....

b Set out the procedure for each and indicate how variations in flavour can be introduced to the various products you have chosen.

....

....

....

....

....

....

11 A reception for 350 guests is being held from 6.30 to 8.30 pm. Hot and cold canapés have been ordered. The hot canapés include: savoury patties of salmon, chicken and mushroom; bouchées of lobster, crab and ham; mini pizzas and hamburgers; various foods on skewers; fried fish goujons and fried fish balls. Set out a schedule of the cooking times for the various items and how they would be cooked and served.

12   You have been asked to suggest some original ideas for canapés to be prepared. Draft out a list to be offered to a potential customer.

....

....

....

....

13   Which methods of cooking would you use for the following and why?
     Chicken galantines:

....

....

     Ballottines of duck:

....

....

14   Discuss why whole cooked joints form an important part of cold buffets.

....

....

15   To obtain the maximum quality of appearance and presentation, describe how the following should be cooked.
     20 kg (40 lb) roast turkey:

....

....

     A York ham:

....

....

Roast suckling pig:

....

....

16 What are the dangers in the cooking of whole stuffed fish?

....

....

17 Describe in detail how whole stuffed fish should be cooked.

....

....

....

18 What are the options for the cooking liquid to be used when cooking whole stuffed fish?

....

....

19 Describe in detail how you would cook 500×100 g (4 oz) portions of salmon for serving cold.

....

....

....

....

20 Describe fully the cooking of a whole 10 kg (20 lb) salmon.

....

....

....

....

21 You are required to cook 4 × 2 kg (4 lb) live crabs and 100 × 300 g (12 oz) lobsters for service cold at lunch. When and how would you cook them? Give reasons for your answer and state the cooking times.

....

....

....

....

22 250 portions of cold roast chicken and ham are required for lunch. You have been supplied with York hams previously soaked and 70 ×1½ kg (3 lb) chicken. When and how would you cook the ham and roast the chickens? Give reasons for your answer.

....

....

....

....

....

....

....

....

....

23 Suggest three items for a cold buffet suitable for cooking by each of the following methods.
  Boiling:

....

....

Poaching:

....

....

Steaming:

....

....

Roasting:

....

....

Baking:

....

....

24 Give the approximate cooking time and procedure for buffet preparation of ox tongue.

....

....

3F9.3 *Finish and decorate cold buffet items*

1 Discuss current trends that you have observed in the finishing and decorating of cold buffet items.

....

....

One of the skills of finishing and decorating cold buffet items is in the combination of different flavours, colours and textures used for presentation.

2   Describe fully three items which you consider highlight the skill mentioned.

   ....

   ....

   ....

3   Describe any three items that you have observed which in your opinion do not show this skill and give your reasons why.

   ....

   ....

   ....

4   Although there is scope for personal variation, there are certain appropriate sauces, garnishes and glazes for various buffet products. Complete the following table.

Item	Sauce	Garnish	Glaze
Whole salmon	Mayonnaise	Cucumber, lettuce hearts, tomato segments	Light fish aspic or leave plain
Cold lobster			
Dressed crab			
Fish mousse			
Cold turkey			
Whole sliced roast beef			
Haunch of venison			

5 What are the storage/holding requirements and ideal conditions for finished buffet items and what precautions should be taken when storing the following?

Canapés unglazed:

....

....

Canapés glazed with aspic:

....

....

Compound salads in dressings:

....

....

Sliced meat:

....

....

Glazed ox tongue:

....

....

6 List the various types of socles and any other forms of decorations.

....

....

....

7 Suggest when it is appropriate to use socles, how they are made and give examples for the use of each.

....

....

8   Summarise the health and safety legislation relating to cold buffet work.

....

....

....

9   Many cases of food poisoning have been caused by food served on cold buffets. A sound knowledge of food hygiene and of the relevant food hygiene legislation is therefore essential. Set out a food hygiene code of practice to be displayed in the larder.

....

....

....

....

....

....

10   List the incidents of bad practice in food hygiene that you have observed.

....

....

....

11   Assuming that you are in charge of the larder with several assistants, how would you ensure that the cleanliness of cooking areas and equipment is fully maintained throughout the service in accordance with relevant legislation? Set out your answer in a form suitable for printing and posting on the larder wall.

....

....

....

....

....

....

12 Customers who order cold food items and cold buffets often have personal
    requirements that may call for adjustments to some of your recipes. What should be
    your attitude to this type of situation and why? Support your answer with examples.

....

....

....

....

13 Name a number of items suitable to form a cold buffet for 100 people for Boxing Day
    lunch and indicate how you would maximise the quality by the finishing and
    methods of decoration.

....

....

....

....

....

14 Quote relevant legislation concerning the storage of finished and decorated products
    not required for immediate consumption, taking into account recipe specifications.

....

....

....

15 Discuss the following: 'The decoration of cold buffet items should be attractive, artistic, simple and kept to the minimum.' Support your answer with examples.

....

....

....

16 Why and how can over-decoration and elaboration of cold buffet items be dangerous with regard to food hygiene? It is also labour intensive and costly. Support your answer with examples that you have observed.

....

....

....

....

17 You are required to produce 750 plated portions of assorted smoked fish. Name your selection, and explain how you would time, plate and serve them.

....

....

....

18 Name twelve varied canapés and describe how you would finish each one.

....

....

....

....

....

....

19 Many pâtés are made without a pastry case.
    a Name two such pâtés.

....

    b Indicate how you would display them on a buffet.

....

....

    c State how you would present a plated portion.

....

....

20 Name eight appetising compound salads. Give the ingredients and dressing for each.

....

....

....

....

....

....

....

21 Name four individual salad items suitable for the buffet.

....

....

22 What salad dressings should be available on the buffet?

....

....

23 Describe how you would decorate (if necessary) and present:
Cold crab mousse:

....

....

Cold ham mousse:

....

....

24 Suggest how you would finish and present:
A dish of 10 portions of chicken ballottines:

....

....

A dish of 10 portions of duck ballottines:

....

....

25 List the procedures and reasons for using aspic jelly.

....

....

....

26 Name four items you consider are improved by the addition of aspic.

....

....

27 What are the dangers associated with aspic jelly?

....

28 Name four whole joints suitable for cold buffets.

....

....

29 Describe how you would prepare and present each joint.

....

....

....

....

30 Describe how you would finish and present:
   1 × 10 kg (20 lb) whole salmon:

....

....

   50 individual portions of salmon in services of 10:

....

....

   500 plated portions of salmon:

....

....

   What sauce(s) and accompaniments (if any) would you offer?

....

....

31 Suggest one pastry encased meat and one pastry enclosed fish item suitable for the buffet.

....

a Describe how you would present them whole.

....

....

b Describe how you would present them in portions.

....

....

32 You have been requested to dress and serve a cold buffet for 450 people in May at 2 pm. The customer has requested pre-portioned first courses (a choice of three), to be followed by whole salmon and whole joints (a choice of four) to be carved/portioned from the buffet, accompanied by an interesting choice of simple and compound salads. No aspic or chaudfroid are to be used.
a Name and describe your choice of dishes.

....

....

....

....

....

....

....

....

....

....

....

....

....

....

b What would be your estimate of the number of carvers required?

....

33 You are required to produce a high-quality cold buffet for 250 in October at 8 pm. The customer has requested an attractively decorated buffet. Using this space as the buffet table, draw outlines indicating the various dishes you have chosen and write the names either inside or beside the outlines. Include all salads, dressings and accompaniments.

34 Various ethnic styles of food are becoming increasingly popular. List some examples for:

Appetisers:

....

....

Canapés:

....

....

Fish dishes:

....

....

Poultry dishes:

....

....

Meat dishes:

....

....

Vegetarian dishes:

....

....

Salads:

....

....

Record of Achievement – Completion of Unit 3F9

Candidate's signature   ....

Assessor's signature   ....

Date   ....
